Cosmic Conflict

Understanding Spiritual Warfare

by
B. E. Underwood
and
Stuart Kelly

The following abbreviations are used to denote other versions:

KJV = *King James Version* of the Bible

RSV = *Revised Standard Version* of the Bible, © 1946, 1952 and 1971, 1973 by the Division of Christian Education of the National Council of Churches of Christ in the U.S.A.

NEB = *The New English Bible*, © 1961, 1970 by the Delegates of the Oxford University Press and the Syndics of the Cambridge University Press

JB = *The Jerusalem Bible*, © 1966, 1967, and 1968 by Darton, Longman & Todd Ltd. and Doubleday & Company, Inc.

Phillips = *The New Testament in Modern English*, Revised Edition, © 1958, 1959, 1960, 1972 by J. B. Phillips

Peterson = *The Message: The New Testament in Contemporary English*, © by Eugene Peterson

LB = *The Living Bible*, © 1971 by Tyndale House Publishers

Published by LifeSprings Resources
P.O. Box 9
Franklin Springs, GA 30639

Printed in the United States of America
ISBN 0-91186-629-9

Table of Contents

Foreword

There has been a flood of books on spiritual warfare published during the past decade. Many of these books have provided fresh insights into the subject. Some have created controversy and confusion in the body of Christ. I deeply appreciate some of the leaders in this emphasis on the subject.

The development of the material in this book has been a lifetime experience. During 55 years of ministry I have learned the importance of "knowing the enemy" and of knowing how to use the armor provided the saint. As the subject of spiritual warfare has been expanded, I have seen Christian soldiers who seem to know more about "advanced weaponry" than they do about the basics of warfare. They are like raw recruits trying to use Scud missiles.

So, the material in this book was developed to provide a basic understanding of biblical teaching concerning our warfare. As I have taught these truths, many people have expressed appreciation for the insights they received into the fundamentals of cosmic conflict. While the themes are basic, I trust that the readers will receive fresh understanding of the issues involved.

Thanks to many people for their help and encouragement. Thelma McDowell, my secretary, Shirley Spencer, editor of publications for LifeSprings Resources, Charlene West, and Dr. Garnet Pike, dean of the Graduate School at Southwestern College of Christian Ministries. All of these read and helped to edit the manuscript.

Special thanks to my friend, Stuart Kelly. He popularized the material and took some of the "preachiness" out of it. Plus he has added much to the final draft of the book. This book is really a joint project between the two of us. I am delighted to co-author the material with him.

— B. E. Underwood

Acknowledgement

Life often seems to run in circles.

Three decades ago as a 14-year-old, I did battle on the basketball courts of Dublin, Virginia, with B. E. Underwood. From him I learned a lot about warfare (not the spiritual kind). In addition, his son Paul was my best buddy, and when the two of us weren't shooting hoops, we conducted night-time guerrilla raids on our friends and on the nearby church camp swimming pool, mostly when our parents were asleep. Those were exhilarating days.

A few years later B.E.'s preaching and teaching helped mentor me as a young pastor. His ministry deepened my grasp and gratitude for the power of God's Word and the marvel of God's grace.

We also shared grimmer moments. B.E. preached at the funerals for my father, M. D. Kelly, and my sister, Trula Harrell. Dealing with those losses and the resulting crisis in my faith was as intense a time of spiritual warfare as I've known.

Now the circle is completed with this book. Teaming up for this project has been just as much fun as those long-ago basketball skirmishes (and much less painful). I'm sure Dad and Trula would be pleased. To the two of them, who've completed their active duty and rest at kingdom headquarters awaiting the final victory, I dedicate my efforts.

Final victory … that will complete the greatest circle of all.

— *Stuart Kelly*

Introduction

Christians are at war.

We're engaged in the mother of all battles. Bigger than any conflict ancient or modern. Greater than World War II. More far-reaching than the fictional **Star Wars** or the hypothetical World War III.

This clash uses weaponry and tactics never imagined by any movie scriptwriter or any military strategist. It includes every nation, every race, every person on the planet. The fate of the whole universe hangs on the outcome of this contest.

It is the cosmic confrontation between God and Satan. Between the King of light and the prince of darkness. Between the forces of good and the legions of evil. It is war beyond all wars, the stuff from which all other hostilities derive.

It is spiritual warfare.

The battle has raged for eons, ever since that traitor Lucifer rebelled against God's rule and was hurled from heaven. This titanic struggle has bloodied humanity ever since the ancient serpent seduced the susceptible couple with the slanderous, "Has God said . . . ?" From intimidation to imitation, from materialism to maliciousness, from the deceptive to the demonic, Satan has cooked up every imaginable chaos among God's creation in an attempt to upend His authority.

That's why this book is written:

1) So you can better understand the devil and his tactics. You need to know who he is, where he came from, how he operates, and where he's headed.

2) So you will know beyond question who is going to win the biggest of all wars. The outcome has never been in doubt. Satan has already met his Waterloo. *The rest of the story* has been written, and the script is just waiting to be played out.

3) So you will know where you fit into the battle. God's going to win, but we must serve like valiant soldiers if we're to share in His triumph and not become casualties of the fray.

We must practice heaven's battle tactics and develop a *boot camp spirituality* to experience victory on the front lines of spiritual struggle.

The bad news is that Christians are in the middle of a huge war.

The good news is that we're going to win.

There are two equal and opposite errors into which our race can fall about the devils. One is to disbelieve in their existence. The other is to believe and to feel an excessive and unhealthy interest in them. They themselves are equally pleased by both errors.

— *C. S. Lewis*

When I was converted, I made this mistake: I thought the battle was already won, the crown already in my grasp. I thought the old things had passed away, that all things had become new, and that my old corrupt nature, the old life, was gone. But I found out, after serving Christ for a few months, that conversion was only like enlisting in the army—that there was a battle on hand.

— *D. L. Moody*

1

Call to Battle

Two boys were playing. As they romped, one asked the other, "Do you think the devil is real?"

"Of course not," the other retorted. "The devil is just like Santa Claus. It's your daddy."

Many secular folks are like that boy. They scoff at the existence of a personal devil.

In 1982 *Newsweek* wrote about the persistence of evil and the renewed interest in Satan ("Giving the Devil His Due," 8/30/82). The writers correctly identified the symptoms. "Despite the high promise of science, technology and the other tribal gods of the modern era, evil persists on a truly awesome scale."

Unfortunately, the writers' diagnosis missed the mark. "For most people, however, the existence of the Devil is an inadequate explanation for such demonic realities as war, poverty, mass starvation and the possibility of nuclear annihilation .... A trivial personification is hardly adequate to symbolize the mystery of evil that even nonbelievers must confront."

Even some believers disbelieve. Hollywood takes the devil more seriously than many Christians, as the spate of horror movies in recent years with occultic or satanic themes demonstrates. Unfortunately, many of those films promote silly and superficial distortions of evil incarnate. Meanwhile, to a modern, technologically sophisticated Church, computers and church growth strategies often seem more real than dark and demonic forces.

Ponder lines from the Keith and Melody Green song, "No One Believes in Me Anymore" (*For Him Who Has Ears To Hear*, Sparrow Records, 1977):

I'm gainin' power by the hour,
They're fallin' by the score.
You know it's gettin' very simple now
Since no one believes in me anymore.

I used to have to sneak around,
But now they just open their doors.
No one's watchin' for my tricks
Since no one believes in me anymore.

Oh, my job keeps gettin' easier
As day slips into day;
The magazines, the newspapers
Print every word I say.
This world is just my spinnin' top,
It's all like child's play.
You know, I dream that it will never stop,
But I know that it's not that way.

Still my work goes on and on,
Always stronger than before.
I'm gonna make it dark before the dawn
Since no one believes in me anymore.

The Cosmic Conflict

The truth is that the rampant, hideous evil in our world stems from a source far more powerful than someone's daddy. No human ingenuity could conjure up that much depravity and destruction. While each person bears responsibility for his/her individual wrongs, a more potent and pathological presence lies behind the problem of human wickedness. Orchestrating the onslaught is a fiendish field general called Satan.

While many moderns may not accept that, the Bible doesn't blink at spelling evil *d-e-v-i-l.* Ask Jesus whether he believed in a personal prince of darkness. Ask Job. Ask Peter. Ask John, the exiled author of the awesome *Revelation.*

Ask Paul. At the close of Ephesians the apostle capsules the cosmic collision between right and wrong. The epistle's purpose is to explain God's plan for rescuing humanity from sin's clutches. Chapter one tells us that God predestined before the world began that people would be called out in His name and transformed. Chapter two describes the transformation: the spiritually dead come to life by grace through faith. Chapter three details the vast riches of that grace. Chapter four paints a portrait of the Church—Christ's "body"—all those who have come to life and are growing more and more into Christlikeness.

The last of chapter four through the first part of chapter six depicts the lifestyle and common destiny of those who've risen to new life through Christ's grace. They live out a different ethos as they await Christ's return for a Church without stain, wrinkle, or any blemish. He gave His life to make that Church a perfect gift for Himself. He will come back to claim His gift. Not even the gates of hell can stop it.

So far everything sounds great. Halfway through chapter six, however, storm clouds form on the horizon. A chill invades the air. The booming of artillery and drone of aircraft are heard in the distance.

Paul's final lines remind us that we're fighting a war. Satan, God's arch-enemy, furious at his former Master's success in salvaging His ruined creation, is determined to spoil the Almighty's redemption strategy. Because of who we are in Christ, what we have, and where we're bound, we've inherited a role in God's cosmic conflict. We face an opponent hell-bent on preventing us from becoming the mature sons of God that He has ordained us to be.

Be Strong

So in 6:10-20 Paul sounds the battle call. He alerts us that a vicious fight rages and warns us to prepare for it. His message from headquarters commands us to "be strong in the Lord and in his mighty power" (v. 10).

Why such a warning? Why such strong language as we prepare for battle?

1) *Because our enemy is so strong.* The devil is no 90-pound weakling. The Bible portrays him as a formidable foe. As a

"strong man" (Luke 11:21). As a roaring lion who prowls about looking for prey to devour (1 Peter 5:8). As a fallen archangel who packs such a wallop that not even another archangel, Michael, dared tackle him on his own, but rebuked him in the name of the Lord (Jude 9).

The "god of this age" (2 Corinthians 4:4) and "prince of the power of the air" (Ephesians 2:2, *KJV*) outmatches any human being. I've met believers who viewed Satan as a paper tiger and thought they could snatch him by the scruff of the neck and shake him like a rag doll. Such an underestimate of his might is naive and dangerous.

Remember the seven sons of Sceva (Acts 19:11-16)? They had watched Paul cast out demons and decided to start a copycat ministry. Using his formula they confronted a demon-possessed fellow. He responded, "I know Jesus and Paul, but you don't scare me a bit." Then he thrashed them.

In "A Mighty Fortress Is Our God," Martin Luther tells it like it is:

For still our ancient foe doth seek to work us woe;
His craft and power are great, and, armed with cruel hate,
On earth is not his equal.

2) *Because we are so weak.* Like a drunk man who thinks he can whip everyone in the county, Christians can become intoxicated with their own power. They not only underestimate the enemy's strength but overestimate their own. In fact, one of the deceiver's favorite tricks is to lull us into overconfidence.

Humanity at its best, however, is outgunned by the evil one. Adam and Eve, perfect human beings, slipped into Satan's snare. Mighty saints such as David and Peter tumbled when they relied on their own resources. Even Jesus conquered temptation in the wilderness by relying on the supernatural weapons of Word and Spirit. "If you think you are standing firm," Paul warns, "be careful that you don't fall" (1 Corinthians 10:12).

Do you know why so many pastors and church leaders become fallen heroes? They mistakenly conclude they can handle temptation on their own. They fail to see their vulnerability and need for divine help.

3) *Because God is so mighty.* Luther's song continues:

> Did we in our own strength confide, our striving would be losing;
> Were not the right man on our side, the Man of God's own choosing.
> Dost ask who that may be? Christ Jesus, it is He;
> Lord Sabaoth His name, from age to age the same,
> And He must win the battle.

The real war is between God and the fallen rebel, Lucifer. Christians take up arms because we've sworn allegiance to heaven's flag. But this is God's war, not ours. And God never loses a war.

When the time was right, God launched His D-Day invasion, planting His own Son undercover behind enemy lines. Philip Yancey describes it this way (*The Jesus I Never Knew*, Zondervan, 1995):

> Revelation 12 pulls back the curtain to give us a glimpse of Christmas as it must have looked from somewhere far beyond Andromeda ... It pictures a dragon leading a ferocious struggle in heaven. A woman clothed with the sun and wearing a crown of 12 stars cries out in pain as she is about to give birth. Suddenly, the enormous red dragon enters the picture, his tail sweeping a third of the stars out of the sky and flinging

> them to the earth. He crouches hungrily before the woman, eager to devour her child the moment it is born. At the last second, the infant is snatched away to safety, the woman flees into the desert, and all-out cosmic war begins ....
>
> Two parallel histories occur simultaneously ... On earth, a baby was born, a king got wind of it, a chase ensued. In heaven, the Great Invasion had begun, a daring raid by the ruler of the forces of good into the universe's seat of evil.

Jesus trounced the adversary on His own turf. He sabotaged Satan at every turn. The God-man learned and grew in perfect obedience. He liberated people's imprisoned bodies, minds, and spirits through His miracles and teachings. To borrow His own metaphor, Jesus entered the strong man's house, tied him up, and made off with his possessions (Matthew 12:29).

Paradoxically Christ's triumph over the forces of evil climaxed with His humiliating death on the cross. There He conquered the wicked one once and for all. "He forgave us all our sins, having canceled the written code with all its regulations, that was against us and that stood opposed to us; he took it away, nailing it to the cross. And having disarmed the powers and authorities, he made a public spectacle of them, triumphing over them by the cross" (Colossians 2:13-15).

What a victory! The Seed of the woman bruised the serpent's head and robbed him of all his illicit spoils. Like an ancient conqueror parading his chained foe through city streets, God wants everyone to know His triumph is total and irreversible. The risen Christ now holds the keys of death and hades (Revelation 1:18), and He extends to us His clout. "I have given you authority to trample on snakes and scorpions and to overcome all the power of the enemy," Jesus told the disciples (Luke 10:19). "Nothing will harm you." "If God is for us, who can be against us?" the Bible reasons. "In all these things we are more than conquerors through him who loved us" (Romans 8:31, 37).

The Battle Is God's

The key to our victory, then, is this: recognizing the battle is not ours but God's. On our own we cannot fend off Satan's attacks. God has already crushed the kingdom of darkness, though, and promises to fight for us.

We see that in the tale of Judah's invasion by a huge army of Moabites, Ammonites and Edomites (2 Chronicles 20). A frantic King Jehoshaphat called on the whole nation to fast and seek God's help. As they prayed, the Spirit came upon a Levite named Jahaziel. He then addressed the worried king and assembled crowd.

"King Jehoshaphat, I have a word from the Lord," Jahaziel began. "Do not be afraid or discouraged because of this vast army. For the battle is not yours, but God's." Jahaziel went on to explain that Judah's soldiers wouldn't even need to fight, but would serve as spectators while the Lord wiped out their antagonists.

When we Christians grasp this truth, we lose our fear of losing the war against evil. It's God's campaign. If we remain on His side, we're sure to win.

A young David understood that. When he took on gargantuan Goliath (1 Samuel 17), he knew he was merely a kid, less equipped to fight than his brothers or any of the other recruits in Israel's military. He knew something else, though, which everyone else seemed to have forgotten. He knew God. He realized the issues involved, and who Israel's Commander-in-chief was. In that awareness he found great courage.

When David reached the battlefield where the Israelites and

Philistines had faced off, he discovered something terribly wrong. He saw men dressed like soldiers, armed like soldiers, talking like soldiers. But they weren't fighting like soldiers. They had been scared out of their sandals by Goliath's challenge. They had ceased being God's warriors and had become hand-wringing onlookers. Like some churches.

David couldn't handle that. "It's not right for this uncircumcised Philistine to defy God's army," he fretted. "I will fight him and God will deliver me from his hand. God is on my side." Tough talk, sure, but backed up by a tough faith.

Approaching the cursing, taunting giant, David tossed some verbal barbs of his own. "This day the Lord will hand you over to me, and I'll strike you down and cut off your head. I'm going to feed the Philistines' carcasses to the birds and wild animals, and the whole world will know there is a God in Israel. Everyone gathered here will know that sword and spear don't win the fight; FOR THE BATTLE IS THE LORD'S."

You know what happened next. David tossed more than barbs, Goliath ended the day a head shorter, the Philistines were routed, and Israel learned an invaluable lesson in waging spiritual warfare.

That lesson remains relevant. Christians needn't adopt a defensive posture. We are to take the offensive, pursuing the enemy and plundering him. An army doesn't win a war by defending but by attacking. God has not called us to hold the fort but to storm the strongholds of the devil. God is on the offensive, invading Satan's territory and reclaiming what he has stolen.

Before World War II, the French built the Maginot Line, a system of heavy fortifications designed to protect the nation from invasion. The Nazi blitzkrieg, however, merely skirted the line, and soon Hitler's soldiers controlled France. The great line of defense proved useless.

God's people aren't meant to cower, wring their hands, or hold the line. The battle is the Lord's. In His strength we're dispatched as part of heaven's invasion to storm the beaches, parachute behind enemy lines, and infiltrate the opposition. *Onward, Christian Soldiers* should be our marching theme.

We take crucial *top-secret* information with us into the fight. We know that God has promised to crush the serpent's head (Genesis 3:15). That the Mighty One has amassed a great army of saints around the world. That the Lord leads the clash against the rebel prince of darkness. That our Father's power shields us from harm (1 Peter 1:5). That an army of angels serves on our side (Hebrews 1:14, Matthew 26:53). That God's limitless power lives within us (Ephesians 3:20). That God is for us (Romans 8:31), with us (Matthew 1:23), and in us (Philippians 2:12, 13).

With all that intelligence data at our disposal, we should be ready to advance fearlessly.

Soldierly Advice

Christian warrior, memorize these five principles and carry them with you into the war zone:

1) *Don't be surprised.* It's war. Anything can happen. "Do not be surprised at the fiery ordeal which comes upon you to prove you, as though something strange were happening to you" (1 Peter 4:12, RSV). Don't let Satan's tactics shake you.

2) *Don't be frightened.* Much of the literature on spiritual warfare either overestimates or underestimates the devil's might, and almost invariably underrates God. The prince of darkness is powerful but not all-powerful. John assures his readers that "the one who is in you is greater than the one who is in the world" (1 John 4:4). The Bible urges us to flee certain things but never tells us to run from the evil one.

3) *Don't be half-hearted.* If you're going to fight, get after it. Give Christ all you've got (Mark 12:30; 1 John 2:4). In high school the football coach would say, "Hit hard! Those who get hurt usually are those who hit halfway. If you'll attack the ball carrier with everything you have, you're less likely to be injured."

4) *Don't retreat.* The word "stand" in Ephesians 6: 11: means to hold the territory that you already have. Hold your ground. Don't budge an inch. "Stand firm in one spirit, contending as one man for the faith of the gospel without being frightened in any way by those who oppose you. This is a sign to them that they will be destroyed, but that you will be saved—and that by God" (Philippians 1:27, 28).

5) *Don't fall asleep.* "Be vigilant," Peter cautions. Stay wide-awake. *Watch!* is the repeated watchword of the New Testament. Don't live like a sleepy or drunken person. (1 Thessalonians 5:6, 7). Remain spiritually alert and self-controlled.

Another football man, Bum Phillips, colorful and down-home coach of the Houston Oilers, was known for his unconventional appearance. He used to stroll the side-lines in flattop haircut, jeans, and snakeskin western boots.

He was also known for his drawling one-liners. Once he spoke admiringly of another pro coach, the Miami Dolphins' Don Shula. "He can take his'n and beat your'n," Phillips mused. "He can also take your'n and beat his'n."

That's our God. Arrange the chess pieces on the board any way you wish. Make the odds as long as your arm. Paint Him into the tiniest corner. The Omnipotent One will still pull out the victory.

Yes, the devil does exist.

But the battle belongs to the Lord.

Some men get so caught up in their own holiness that they look at the Trinity for a possible vacancy.

—John MacArthur

God is looking for men in whose hands his glory is safe.

—A. W. Tozer

2

Son of the Morning

A cartoon years ago depicted a dainty, elderly woman exiting the Sunday morning service. As she greets her pastor she comments, "That sermon was very nice, Reverend, but some of those things I'd rather not know about until I actually get to hell."

Many Christians adopt a similar attitude toward hell's number one tenant. They seem determined to know as little about Satan and his strategies as possible. Few sermons broach the subject. When preachers do mention the devil, at times they give the impression that they are talking tongue-in-cheek. They treat him as though he were an old folk tale or a humorous myth, rather than a vile, intelligent, powerful personality who commands the legions of darkness.

Mastermind Behind the Mayhem

Open-minded people must admit the fact that God's

kingdom faces strategic, organized opposition. Such "business" as murder and mayhem, crime and corruption, cults and the occult, child abuse and sexual abuse, drugs and demonism, selfishness and sensualism, pride and prejudice presuppose a malevolent mastermind. The threads of evil aren't woven by chance. The supernatural resistance the Church encounters isn't coincidental. Tragically too many believers remain clueless to the tyrant's tools of trade.

Perhaps one reason for our relative ignorance is the devil's *modus operandi.* He generally works undercover. Incognito. The wizard of wickedness is spirit, not body. At least on this earth he has no physical manifestation except through other creatures. Which generally suits him just fine, thank you, since cunning and deception are chief weapons in his arsenal. Usually the less people realize they're dealing with the devil, the bigger his advantage.

Scripture alerts us to that. Satan is often addressed through other persons or beings. For example, in the garden of Eden (Genesis 3) the Lord doesn't speak to the devil directly, even though he's obviously playing a key role in this moral drama. Instead God talks to the serpent as though it were Satan. If we miss that technique of biblical narration, important truths about him will elude us.

The same phenomenon occurs in the Gospels. In Matthew 16:21-23 Jesus attempts to prepare His disciples for the rugged road ahead. When He mentions His impending suffering and death, however, Simon Peter blows a fuse and tries to correct the Master's thinking. Jesus harshly rebukes him, saying, "Get behind me, Satan."

Christians tend to stumble over that verse. It seems a crude, unfair blast for Jesus to level at one of His own. In reality, the Lord was looking past Simon to the sinister spirit that had prompted Simon's unwitting but dangerous protest. Jesus was also demonstrating for His disciples of all time how easily we can become the devil's accomplice without realizing it.

Isaiah 14 uses a similar approach. It offers a scathing prophecy against the king of Babylon. But by v. 12, the language seems clearly to refer to Satan. By addressing the entity through which the diabolical one was operating—perhaps his greatest tool for wickedness at that time—God spoke indirectly to the devil.

Look behind any evil person on this planet and you'll find Satan's influence. In the theater of human depravity, he directs the scenes from offstage, cues the actors, and supplies many of the props. He works through people. And in the degenerate behavior of human beings, we glimpse Lucifer's own tactics and motives. "You belong to your father, the devil, and you want to carry out your father's desire," Jesus railed at a group of hostile Jews. Like father, like son—in evil also.

Again we find the same pattern in Ezekiel 28. At first the prophet addresses his message to the prince of Tyre. As the prophecy progresses, however, the language leaps into a higher gear. Obviously someone other than a mere human is being confronted.

> The word of the Lord came to me: "Son of man, take up a lament concerning the king of Tyre and say to him: 'This is what the Sovereign Lord says:
>
> "'You were the model of perfection,
> full of wisdom and perfect in beauty.
> You were in Eden,
> the garden of God;
> every precious stone adorned you:
> ruby, topaz and emerald,
> chrysolite, onyx and jasper,
> sapphire, turquoise and beryl.

Your settings and mountings were made of gold;
on the day you were created they were prepared.
You were anointed as a guardian cherub,
for so I ordained you.
You were on the holy mount of God;
you walked among the fiery stones.
You were blameless in your ways
from the day you were created
till wickedness was found in you.
Through your widespread trade
you were filled with violence,
and you sinned.
So I drove you in disgrace from the mount of God,
and I expelled you, O guardian cherub,
from among the fiery stones.
Your heart became proud
on account of your beauty,
and you corrupted your wisdom
because of your splendor.
So I threw you to the earth;
I made a spectacle of you before kings.
By your many sins and dishonest trade
you have desecrated your sanctuaries.
So I made a fire come out from you,
and it consumed you,
and I reduced you to ashes on the ground
in the sight of all who were watching.'"
(Ezekiel 28:11-18)

The Brightest and Best

We don't know all about the evil one that our curiosities wish for. Careful study of texts as richly suggestive as this, however, sheds a great deal of light.

Here, better than anywhere in the Bible, you can gaze on a portrait of Satan before his fall. And what a stunning picture you find. The archfiend's name then was Lucifer, which meant *son of the morning*. Or *son of light*. Or *son of the dawn*.

This passage, coupled with others, suggests that Lucifer was the brightest, most beautiful creature in heaven. No other spiritual being except God approached the brilliance, the splendor of this angel. Ezekiel describes him as robed in every variety of precious stone. Picture someone dressed head to foot in glittering, shimmering, light-capturing jewels—emeralds, rubies, sapphires and every other dazzling decoration.

Lucifer was full of beauty. The epitome of wisdom. Perfect in every way. If we could have glimpsed him before his fall, we would have beheld the most splendid, magnificent being God could create.

Until you peruse this portrait, until you understand Satan's surpassing glory and ability, you cannot appreciate what spiritual warfare involves. Often we imagine him as some dark, morbid creature with horns and long tail, fire blasting from his nostrils—a weird, medieval caricature. In these verses, though, he's depicted as a being of incredible loveliness, grace, and intelligence. Understanding who he was helps us grasp who he is. Knowing what he had explains the rage he feels over what he's lost. Seeing the tremendous influence for good he wielded gives us respect for the great force of evil he has become.

Apparently all of heaven's legions looked up to Lucifer. He was God's right-hand angel, the Lord's messenger. Ezekiel calls him "the anointed cherub." Cherubim protected the glory cloud of Jehovah. Lucifer therefore served as guardian of God's throne. He resided on the "holy mount of God" and strolled among "the fiery stones," symbols that suggest great authority and intimacy with God.

From Ezekiel's picturesque words we can visualize Lucifer's heavenly ministry focusing on three areas:

1) ***He was a prophet.*** A prophet speaks for God. Lucifer functioned as God's mouthpiece, proclaiming the Almighty's messages to the heavenly host. All the angels knew that what Lucifer uttered were God's own words. He must have been privy to some of his Sovereign's most majestic and secret plans. Did the devil know and proclaim to the angelic legions Yahweh's grand design for this earth? We can only wonder.

Here lies a truth, by the way, that should do wonders for those who preach. God calls people like us—finite, fallible folks—to stand before eternal souls and be His spokespersons. To proclaim, "Thus says the Lord …," is an awesome reality that ought to heighten our humility and self-esteem both at the same time. It's the job of all jobs, as the now-prince of darkness once knew.

2) ***He was a priest.*** Ezekiel 28:13b is rendered in the KJV "the workmanship of thy tabrets and of thy pipes was prepared in thee in the day that thou wast created." The marginal reading says, "tambourines and flutes." The implication is that instruments of music were built into his very nature. Is it any wonder that music is one of his most effective weapons against the kingdom of God?

He led the worship in heaven as the anointed cherub who ministered in the original holy of holies (not the earthly copy that Moses would later construct). Perhaps he was like the high priest in that Old Testament tabernacle who could approach the Most High like no one else could. The anointed cherub standing as sentinel about God's glory cloud—that's as close to God as you can get. In fact, it appears he operated so close to the center of Glory that he began to think he himself was it.

Can that be one reason Satan so despises the Church? It is a worshiping community; that's our most important function as members of Christ's body. Our whole existence is intended to be an act of worship to the Lord (Romans 12:1; 1 Corinthians 10:31). And when we arrive in eternity, we will lead the hosts of heaven in the praise to God that Lucifer abandoned when he fell.

3) ***He was a prince.*** Now he's known as the prince of the power of the air. Then he was a prince in the court of the King of kings. He came and went in the throne room not of the Czar of Russia or the Emperor of Rome but of the Lord of the universe. Ezekiel's description indicates God had delegated to Lucifer tremendous authority. He carried enough clout that, when he rebelled, he persuaded one-third of the angels to follow him. He was no glorified go-fer but was essentially God's second-in-command.

We're confronted with a creature who was awesome in nature (who he was) and in function (what he did). He ministered as a prophet, priest, and prince. It doesn't take an Einstein to look at this portrait and realize this was and is Jesus' ministry. And it will be ours as believers. We will inherit the job description of the Son of the morning. No wonder the apostle Paul dubs us "sons of the light and sons of the day" (1 Thessalonians 5:5) who are to "shine like stars in the universe" (Philippians 2:15), and Jesus urges, "Let your light shine before men, that they may see your good deeds and praise your Father in heaven" (Matthew 5:16).

But we do wonder about one issue. Didn't God know Lucifer would blow it? Didn't the Omniscient see the rebellion coming long before it happened and, if so, why did He allow it? Why did He permit such a Pandora's box of poisons to unleash itself upon the creation? No more perplexing problem has pestered humanity through the centuries than the existence of evil. If God is great and He is good, then why has He permitted such heinous wickedness to exist in our world? Why? Why?

We can't answer that question fully. Shelves and shelves of books attempt to resolve the issue, with varying success. Believers' main consolation over the years has come from the confidence that whatever has happened must be viewed in the light of what yet will happen. The all-powerful, all-wise, all-merciful Maker will remake His fallen creation. What He promises to bring out of this sewer of sin and suffering will so outdo what the devil has devised, that it will more than compensate for all the tragedy that has resulted from the fall.

If God could place His stamp of approval on the original creation ("It is good"), undoubtedly His new creation will also pass muster. What the crowds gushed about Jesus' healings—"He has done everything well" (Mark 7:37)—surely will pour from our awestruck lips when we view history's panorama from God's mountain-top view.

Lucifer once looked down from that mountain. He soared like an eagle among the divine peaks. The dazzle of the sacred, however, is also its danger. Like the Greek myth of Icarus flying too close to the sun, the closer one gets to God's power and glory, the keener the temptation to feel godlike about oneself. The son of the morning flew too high and got burned.

The Terrible Tumble

Satan's dominion became his downfall. One day it dawned on the son of dawn how much power and influence he wielded, and this magnificent creature concluded that he stood on a par with the Creator. He decided the celestial corporation was ripe for a hostile takeover. How easily he would later flip the phrase at Adam and Eve, "Has God said ...?" for it was a voice of insolent challenge he'd first heard within himself.

Satan merchandised his ministry. He prostituted his prophetic office, speaking not for his Lord but for himself. He perverted his priestly status, diverting worship from God unto himself. He pandered his princely rule, bowing to his unbridled ambitions.

Like Narcissus gazing at his reflection in the water, Lucifer became entranced by his own beauty and greatness. "What a shining star I am. Why should the Almighty get all the spotlight? Shouldn't Mr. Majestic myself also command top billing? What do you think, fellows?" It seemed plausible enough, at least to him and to a significant minority of the angelic army. The coup d'etat was conceived.

All the wickedness and deviltry in this world have sprouted from this rebellion. Lucifer's sin was pride, and pride lies at the root of most of our sins. We like to play God. That's fallen humanity's favorite pastime: playing games with our lives and with other people's. Going beyond our legitimate authority. Manipulating our ministry. Straying from our stewardship. Assuming to ourselves clout and credit we don't deserve. It's all rotted fruit from the same twisted tree.

"Nobody has a good excuse," Eugene Peterson paraphrases the first chapter of Romans in *The Message*. "What happened was this: People knew God perfectly well, but when they didn't treat him like God, refusing to worship him, they trivialized themselves into silliness and confusion so that there was neither sense nor direction left in their lives. They pretended to know it all, but were illiterate regarding life (Romans 1:20-22).

Christians not only aren't immune to the Lucifer "virus," we're especially susceptible. To serve God, to possess Spirit-credentialed authority, is to sip a highly intoxicating beverage. Here's how it works. You minister and lives change. You preach or teach or counsel and people listen, listen to you like you're God's own mouthpiece. You begin to get the idea that lives are changing and people are listening because you're something special.

Soon you lose the awe. The rapturous turns routine. Without carefully articulating your thoughts (after all, none of us ever wants to *admit* to playing God), you start seeing yourself as part of the glory rather than just an instrument of it. God's lucky to have someone like you on His staff, you conclude. You should take more of the credit, grab some of the glory for yourself.

Power, even (and maybe especially) spiritual power, is highly seductive.

A year after the PTL debacle, Richard Dortch reflected in *Christianity Today* (3/18/88) on his involvement in the scandal. "A television camera can change a preacher quicker than anything else," he mused. "It turns good men into potentates … It's so easy to get swept away by popularity: everybody loves you, cars are waiting for you, and you go to the head of the line. That's the devastation of the camera. It has made us less than what God has wanted us to become."

Wanting to become more than he was, Lucifer became far less than he had been. When you realize the heights at which Satan stood, you appreciate his fury over the depths to which he has fallen. Why does he despise every disciple of Jesus? Why does our praise of God torment him so? Because it reopens bitter wounds. It drives into his heart the stake of reality: he has lost his glory and will never regain it.

That's why we're at war. That's why the devil is throwing every weapon in his arsenal at us. That's why our pilgrimage to destiny includes so many landmines, snipers, and ambushes. The Christian walk isn't a cakewalk. Our foe is furious and he is formidable.

Do you remember Howard Hughes? For decades he bore

the reputation as one of the world's wealthiest and most powerful men. He wielded influence particularly in the aviation and motion picture industries. His name grew legendary in American society.

Then in the 1950s, he dropped out of sight. Hardly anyone saw him. Those who did lay eyes on the multimillionaire in his later years drew a picture of a paranoid recluse with grossly long fingernails and wild hair, who lived in a darkened bedroom and held a morbid fear of infection. A stranger chancing upon him would never have guessed this disheveled hermit was the rich and notorious Howard Hughes. To appreciate whom he now stood before, an onlooker would have had to understand who this person had been.

So it is with Satan. We envision him, shadowy and mysterious, in his murky underworld existence. We often see little directly of him or his actions. We're told his impact is pervasive, yet that's sometimes hard to believe. To fully appreciate whom we're dealing with—his tormented state, his boiling hatred, his superhuman power, his sophisticated tactics—we must understand the pinnacle from which he fell and the abyss to which he has plummeted.

To defeat the enemy of our souls, we need to appreciate not only who he is. But what he was.

Every man for himself, his own ends, the Devil for all.
—*Robert Burton*

The one principle of hell is "I am my own."
—*George MacDonald*

Nothing burns in hell but self-will ... Hell is nothing but self-will, and if there were no self-will, there would be no devil and no hell.
—*Theologica Germanica*

3

King of the Mountain

What a tragedy!

He had it all. Talent, youth, looks, fame. His 6'8" frame packed an amazing blend of grace and power, speed and coordination. Despite his collegiate success in the prestigious Atlantic Coast Conference and his All-American credentials, his best basketball apparently lay in front of him. Selection in the first-round of the NBA draft by the storied Boston Celtics confirmed his rising stardom.

Tragically, Len Bias never played a single game on Boston Garden's parquet floor. Days after the draft, he died on another floor, the one in his dorm room at the University of Maryland, victim of a cocaine overdose. All that talent, all that potential, all the might-have-beens ....

What a waste!

He too seemed to have it all. He was a walking fine arts curriculum, equally at home on stage or before the easel, cradling a guitar or wielding a pen. His poetry, paintings, and performances stirred friends and strangers alike. He came from a poor family, but a full drama scholarship to a major university appeared to ensure his education and a creative career.

However, Robbie never finished his first year of college. Drugs, alcohol, the wrong crowds, and his own lack of discipline sucked him away. A conversion experience got him back on track temporarily, but theological and moral rationalizations plopped him back into the brier patch. Since then he has drifted from one minimum wage job to another, and from one self-deception to the next. His life has been a tragicomedy of blown chances and squandered talent.

What a tragedy! What a waste!

Satan had it all. Beauty, power, wisdom, status. He was God's *right hand angel*, magnificent and matchless among the heavenly creation. He proclaimed the words of God, led in worship of God, moved about the throne of God. His name, Lucifer, mirrored his majesty: *son of the morning, son of light.*

For him that wasn't enough. He reasoned that he didn't have much at all unless he really did have it *all.* Why speak for God when he could speak for himself? Why worship when he could be worshiped? Why be satisfied with *#2* when he could be *#1*? He began to yearn for the Supreme's job. He lusted after the glory and power that belonged exclusively to the Most High.

Do you remember the child's game, "king of the mountain"? A group of kids pick a tree stump, pile of dirt, or large rock, and one of them stands on top of it. Whoever pushes or pulls the first one off his perch becomes the new king. Then that one is dethroned, and so the game goes. The most important rule: only one person can be king at a time.

How Sin Started

Satan decided to play king of the mountain and usurp God's exclusive role. He concurred with management that there could only be one Supreme Being in the universe, but while agreeing on position, he differed on personnel. To him it was obvious who was the best candidate for the job. Listen to the prophet's inspired recounting of the mutiny (Isaiah 14:12-15):

> How have you fallen from heaven,
> O morning star, son of the dawn!
> You have been cast down to the earth,
> you who once laid low the nations!
> You said in your heart,
> "I will ascend to heaven;
> I will raise my throne
> above the stars of God;
> I will sit enthroned on the mount of assembly,
> on the utmost heights of the sacred mountain.
> I will ascend above the tops of the clouds;
> I will make myself like the Most High."
> But you are brought down to the grave,
> to the depths of the pit.

The prophet delivers this scathing rebuke against the king of Babylon. The language, though, seems clearly designed to go further, to refer in a deeper sense to the inventor of arrogance and treason. Here lies the origin of sin. The devil rebelled against God, igniting a fuse that continues to burn throughout this planet today. In his revolt, we see the sinister seeds of our own seditions.

Satan rebelled against the Lord's rule. Until that point the universe had contained only one will. Lucifer had always acted or spoken in harmony with that sovereign desire. "Thy will be done" was his theme song. Now he chose to inject his own will into the harmonious creation.

When he did, God manifested His might. He crushed the turncoat in an instant, hurling him from his heavenly perch. "I saw Satan fall like lightning from heaven," Jesus would later recall to His followers (Luke 10:18). Zap! Lucifer and one-third of heaven's host had been hurled to the earth. The King of kings stood alone on top of His holy mountain.

The prince was now a pauper. The cherub had turned into a chump. The son of light had become the prince of darkness. His fall was as startling as it was swift.

What a tragedy! What a waste!

Where did he fall? To the earth. That seems the best explanation for the curious language of Genesis 1:2. Surely God, in whom dwells light without any darkness at all, would not have designed something as dismal and chaotic as that scene. The arrival of a fallen traitor, on the other hand, could have caused the confusion described there.

In *Paradise Lost*, John Milton paints this portrait of a prince's plunge:

> Him the Almighty Power
> Hurl'd headlong flaming from th' Ethereal Sky
> With hideous ruin and combustion down
> To bottomless perdition, there to dwell
> In Adamantine Chains and penal Fire …

For those rebellious, here thir Prison ordained
In utter darkness, and thir portion set
As far remov'd from God and light of Heav'n
As from the Center thrice to th' utmost Pole.
O how unlike the place from whence they fell!

Divine Counterattack

Darkness visible? Imagine it like this: the tempter tossed from purest light to most benighted blackness. For a thousand years ... ten thousand years ... ten million years—God only knows how long—the devil dwelt in unrelieved night, in "utter darkness." "Blacker than a hundred midnights down in a cypress swamp," James Weldon Johnson (*God's Trombones*, Viking, 1990) calls it. It was a chilling, inky gloom that could be felt as much as seen, an ebony shroud blanketing the spirit. On the planet for which the Creator held such grand designs (in which perhaps He had intended Lucifer to play a pivotal role), the fallen one existed in exile.

All that happened on earth during that time I cannot say. Perhaps the geologists can help us. At some point, however, the Godhead announced His plan. "We're going right onto Lucifer's turf. We will invade his kingdom of darkness. We will create a replacement for the son of dawn, better than the original, that will worship and serve us and proclaim God's will.

"We will create humanity."

Then God decreed, "Let there be light," and perhaps Lucifer experienced his biggest shock since being bounced from the heavenly realm. He had prowled in the shadows for millennia, and suddenly the blinding brilliance of the Father of lights blazed all around him. The counterattack had begun. Heaven's reclamation of a devil-damaged earth was underway.

That's what this spiritual warfare we're engaged in is all about. God is retaking every inch of ground Satan has stolen.

Unfortunately, the war has grown more complicated during the fray. Man and woman—the Maker's new creation formed in His image—unwittingly swallowed the tempter's hook. A foolish grab for self-fulfillment placed the human race in the rebel camp. It didn't sabotage the Lord's strategy, for He had already planned for that eventuality with a "Lamb slain from the creation of the world" (Revelation 13:8). It did, however, give the devil more ammunition.

There was a contingency Satan hadn't contemplated, however. He had thought that through sin humanity would become his absolute servant. His will would predominate in people's lives over God's will. But human beings are so all-fired independent, so much like the devil themselves as God's creatures, that they're not interested in pleasing anyone but themselves if they can manage it. No longer did just one will reside in the universe. Or two wills. Now millions of wills collided with each other, each carrying out its own insurrection against God after Lucifer's blueprint.

Will Power

What turned the brightest angel into the darkest demon? What platform did the son of light stand upon? What specific acts of traitorism landed him in dire straits?

Isaiah tells us. In his prophecy God Himself confronts heaven's traitor. He's indicted on five counts:

1) *I will ascend to heaven.* I will raise myself to God's level, become equal to Him. *I want God's status.*

2) *I will raise my throne above the stars of God.* I refuse to rule just a part of God's realm. I'm determined to control the whole creation. *I want God's job.*

3) *I will sit enthroned on the mount of assembly, on the utmost heights of the sacred mountain.* The reverence reserved for the Holy One should go to me. *I want God's worship.*

4) *I will ascend above the tops of the clouds.* I will rise beyond the clouds of angels that reflect God's brilliance. *I want God's glory.*

5) *I will make myself like the Most High.* The only thing left, after the previous four, is to become God, to usurp for oneself the very powers and prerogatives of deity. *I want God's essence.*

Notice how this scene foreshadows human fallenness. "The only reason God has put this tree's fruit off-limits to you," the serpent would later chide Eve, "is because he knows that if you eat it, *you will be like God.*" That's the core of every sin, isn't it? To play God, to be like God, to assume for ourselves His authority and will.

It's not accidental that Lucifer's fall hinges on these five *I will's.* Until then, as already noted, the universe had only known one will. Every creature spoke these words, "Thy will be done." Every angel in heaven cried out to God's throne, "Have it Your way, Lord." They basked in God's love, they bowed before His wisdom and might, and none of them had ever contemplated any course of behavior other than joyful submission to their Sovereign.

But now the scene changes. An antithetical will asserted itself, and an alternative ideology and ethos set up shop. *My* replaced *Thy.* "I Surrender All" dropped from first place on heaven's hit charts, crowded out by a catchy tune titled "I've Got To Be Me." Self-serving supplanted serving. Ambition spawned sedition which led to perdition.

Satan stood toe-to-toe and chin-to-chin with his Maker and barked, "Move over, that throne is mine now. I'll be the object of worship. I'll bask in the limelight. I declare myself CEO and chairman of the board. Heaven needs a new superstar, and I'm the brightest beam on the block."

He jettisoned God's prophetic, priestly, and princely roles. He ceased trumpeting God's truth to toot his own horn. He stopped leading the applause and started soliciting it. Instead of giving the King kudos, he presented Him with a coup.

To his everlasting horror, Lucifer discovered that the Lord of Glory wasn't ready to retire. The Almighty does not retreat. The coup would be no picnic. Playing God might be a snap, but becoming God was all uphill. The devil's arm was way too short to box with God. Judgment struck the rebels fast and furiously, and God's own words tell the story best.

"How you have fallen from heaven, O morning star, son of the dawn! You have been cast down to the earth" (Isaiah 14:12). "I drove you in disgrace from the mount of God, and I expelled you, O guardian cherub, from among the fiery stones … I threw you to the earth" (Ezekiel 28:16, 17). "God did not spare angels when they sinned, but sent them to hell, putting them into gloomy dungeons to be held for judgment" (2 Peter 2:4). "These he has kept in darkness, bound with everlasting chains for judgment on the great Day" (Jude 6).

The Mind Battle

Since Satan's insurrection introduced an alternative will, two mindsets have battled for supremacy in this world. Two ways of thinking continually struggle for control of every person. One is the mind of Christ. The other is the mentality of the devil. The battle of the mind is the major front of spiritual warfare.

We appreciate, then, the urgency in Paul's pen as he writes the Philippian believers, "Let this mind be in you, which was also in Christ Jesus" (2:5 KJV). *Adopt the life attitude Jesus demonstrated on earth*, the apostle is saying. *Think of yourself the way He thought about Himself. Let His motivation become your motivation*. That's one mindset.

The other—Satan's—goes like this. *I will do my own thing. I will live as I please. I will answer to no one except myself.* "Better to reign in Hell, than serve in Heav'n," as Milton's

Satan reasons. *I am totally free!*

Sounds delicious, doesn't it?

But it's the biggest lie from the father of lies. Look at where the rebel prince's *freedom* took him. His presumption purchased a one-way ticket out of heaven, straight downhill. He was so bent on worshiping himself that God let him. The punishment fit the crime, as Frederick Buechner's inimitable prose pictures it in *Peculiar Treasures* (Harper & Row, 1979):

> The Bible's blackest villain is known by the Bible's loveliest name, and not by accident either. "How art thou fallen from heaven, O Lucifer, son of the morning!" the prophet Isaiah says (Isaiah 14:12), the point being that it was while he was still at the height of his loveliness that the ugly episode took place.
>
> Lucifer was a leading member of the heavenly chorus that sings Bach around the throne of grace and as such seemed so infinitely removed from all temptation that both to him and to all his fellow angels the very possibility must have seemed ludicrous. Then one day he made the mistake of saying to himself, "Just see how far I have come," with the emphasis on the first person singular, and from there to "Just see how far I can still go" was of course only a hop, skip, and a jump.
>
> When you are one of God's right-hand men, there is clearly only one step further you can go, and with his usual uncanny combination of justice and mercy, God let him go there.
>
> Lucifer was no longer called upon to love anybody except himself or to sing Bach anywhere but in the bathtub or to follow anything or anybody except his own instincts and inclinations. He was given an office with mottoes like *Nobody loves you like yourself* and *Nice*

guys finish last on the walls and was named to the Number One job in charge of everybody else who both then and for all time felt the same way ....

The Gospel of "Me"

Every act of rebellion against God since then has followed the same pattern as Satan's sedition. Every time people ignore God's boundaries or withhold God's worship or conclude that they know better how to run their lives than God knows, Isaiah 14 repeats itself. The crux of sin is idolatrous pride: a mindset that puts self at the center of one's universe. Secular society today thinks it's doing a very modern, innovative thing when it turns its back on God's laws. Instead it's just repeating a tedious and tragic pattern, the roots of which reach back to the dawn of time and a creature known as the *son of the dawn.*

A few years ago someone gave this tongue-in-cheek observation of the increasing individualism and self-obsession in American culture. "First we had a magazine called **Life**. Then we narrowed that down to **People**. Next we limited our interest to just **Us**. Now the newest hot-selling periodical is **Self**." That describes the progression of the disease pretty well, doesn't it? Sin eventually leaves a person imprisoned in a universe of one and strangled by self-worship.

Few hymns hail the haughtiness of fallen humanity better than the poem "Invictus," by William Ernest Henley:

Out of the night that covers me,
Black as the Pit from pole to pole,
I thank whatever gods may be
For my unconquerable soul.

In the fell clutch of circumstance
I have not winced or cried aloud.

Under the bludgeonings of chance
My head is bloody, but unbowed.

Beyond this place of wrath and tears
Looms but the horror of the shade,
And yet the menace of the years
Finds, and shall find, me unafraid.

It matters not how strait the gate,
How charged with punishments the scroll,
I am the master of my fate:
I am the captain of my soul.

Few people would dare express, or even admit to themselves, a philosophy that disdainful and defiant. Yet the world is filled with people who *live* those sentiments. Their attitude and lifestyle spit in the face of God's truth. They're determined to act as they choose. Their will stands supreme. Neither God's nor anyone else's plans will interfere with their intentions. They do not shake their fist at God so much as ignore Him, or nod politely in His direction as they head merrily the opposite way.

Shockingly, many church people fit this description. They steadfastly pursue their own agendas with no regard for the will of God.

"Not everyone who says to me, 'Lord, Lord,' will enter the kingdom of heaven," Jesus cautioned, "but only he who does the will of my Father who is in heaven" (Matthew 7:21). As Eugene Peterson puts it, "My will is my glory; it is also that which gives me the most trouble." The sobering fact is that religious activities and organizations provide great hiding places for unsurrendered wills.

Christian ministries can fall into the same snare. Sleek

buildings, larger numbers, polished sermons, and sophisticated programs can become the ends rather than the means. Before we know it, we're building *our* church rather than *the* Church. Again Richard Dortch comments, "Sometimes I think the Church doesn't know anything about true success. It's all tied to how many stations we have on our network, or how big our building is. It's so easy to lose control, to compromise without realizing it ... We were so caught up in God's work that we forgot about God."

Humankind is the most deluded species in the universe. That's why the Bible speaks so much about blindness. Second Corinthians 4:4 captures it best. "The god of this age has blinded the minds of unbelievers, so that they cannot see the light of the gospel of the glory of Christ, who is the image of God."

Like Len Bias and Robbie, humans think they are in control but are being controlled. They think they are their own masters, but they're as much a slave as any poor soul who was ever purchased off an auction block. They think they're captains of their own souls, while in reality they are rudderless ships blown by the gales toward certain disaster. Lost people live in ignorance and blindness, victimized by the archfiend's mind games.

The Mind of Christ

Is it therefore any surprise that Jesus makes "Thy will be done" the centerpiece of His counterinsurgency? That's the bottom line. Those stones pave the road back from oblivion. The only road. Francis Shaeffer writes (*True Spirituality*, Tyndale House, 1971), "I say there is a battle in the universe, and God is God. Then, if I lack trust, what I am really doing is denying in practice that he has a right, as my God, to use me where he wants in the spiritual battle which exists in the seen and the unseen world."

Jehovah has assembled a mighty army to assist His counter-attack against the powers of darkness, but you can't be part of this victorious assault and remain in rebellion. The military is a dictatorship, not a democracy. Superior officers don't request but command. A soldier's allegiance must be unquestioned, his obedience unwavering. Our Commander in Chief orders believers to saturate their brains with His way of thinking.

How does He think? What is the mind of Christ? Philippians 2:5-8 clues us in. It explains the mentality that marks the good soldier of Jesus Christ.

These verses tell us that the Son of God, who had been one with the Father from eternity, who was perfectly and completely God Himself, made an incredible leap into the void. Emptying Himself of His divine prerogatives, Immanuel joined the human race, an incredible humiliation considering who He was and what humanity had become. He lived His entire life as any person would have to. In fact, the Bible insists He was tempted in every way we are. We don't understand that. Can't explain it. But it's true.

You and I have never faced any enticement that He doesn't appreciate, because He's faced it too. Sexuality, ambition, money, physical and psychological appetites—He felt Lucifer's lure in every arena. The temptation to promote oneself, to ignore others' needs, to become bitter, to seek revenge, to take shortcuts to God's will; Jesus encountered it all *just as we do*. Yet without sin.

He escaped sin because He maintained that self-emptying, servant-living, God-pleasing posture. He became not only a man but one of the least of men in society's estimation, a poor working-class Jew from the cultural backwater of Galilee. As an adult He lived out the role of a servant (*doulos*, literally *slave*). Ultimately Christ humbled Himself to the point of dying a criminal's torturous death. Not because He had to—no army held that power over Him—but because He *chose* to give His life in obedience to His Father.

That's the contrast between the devil's reasoning and the posture of Christ. The satanic mindset brags, "I will, I will, I will!" The Christlike attitude prays, "Thy will, Thy will, Thy will!" The difference between heaven and hell hangs between those two monosyllables: *my* and *Thy*. As C. S. Lewis puts it in *The Great Divorce* (Macmillan, 1945), "There are two kinds of people: those who say to God, 'Thy will be done,' and those to whom God says, 'All right, then, have it your way.'"

Remember that the Father is on our side. He created us and therefore knows even better than we do what's best for us. He yearns more than anyone for us to reach our full potential. But God also knows our ministries, our jobs, our families, our churches, and our lives will never be all they're intended to be until we offer God our blank check of surrender. Until then we're unbroken horses, packed with promise but untamed and useless.

Two wills. Two worlds. Two ways of living. One will alone had existed in the universe until part of God's creation in heaven, and then on earth, broke ranks. Now the cosmos lies in chaos like shards of a broken mirror.

But the time is coming, the Bible assures us, when the will of the Eternal One shall reign again without dissent. When every knee shall bow. When every corner of creation—in heaven, on earth, even under the earth—will acknowledge God's sovereignty. When every voice will unanimously cry, "Your will be done." When He who became lower than all for our sake is exalted above all.

We don't have to wait until then, however. We can choose to bow the knee and submit the will to the Most High now. God's kingdom, His royal rule, can flourish within us. We can undergo a spiritual brain transplant as the mind of Christ takes control of our attitudes and actions.

We can crown Him King of the mountain … and of our lives.

He had it all. Unlimited power, total knowledge, absolute freedom, perfect beauty. Whatever He desired, He possessed. Whatever He spoke happened. He lived in perfect harmony with all of heaven's inhabitants, and they adored Him as God. No one could have expected Him to leave all that, to dive into the cesspool of human depravity and rescue a race of creatures who didn't deserve to be rescued.

Yet Jesus did. In stark contrast to the son of light who had asserted his rights above even God's, the Light of the World abandoned His status. He became like us so that incredibly we might become like Him. The King of the mountain became a slave in the valley.

All through His menial existence, even when facing the heaviness of the world's sins and the horror of separation from the Father, the Savior continually breathed the deepest longing of His obedient heart, "Not what I want, but what You want." Somehow His selflessness broke the chains of human selfishness and began to unravel Satan's web of deceit.

What a victory! What a love!

What a God!

Satan's most successful maneuver in churches and Christian organizations is to get people angry at one another, to entice us to attack and insult our brothers and sisters, thus splitting the body of Christ.

— James Dobson

The devil is like a mad dog that is chained up. He is powerless to harm us when we are outside his reach, but once we enter his circle, we expose ourselves again to injury or harm.

—Aurelius Augustine

4 The Evil Empire

It's an old trick. You take a cat that's minding its own business and fling it onto a dog that's doing the same. Now if that canine and feline had enough sense, they'd bite and scratch the living daylights out of you, their common tormentor. Instead they go after each other and fight like, well, cats and dogs, oblivious to the real antagonist who's observing the scene with devilish glee.

A couple of years ago *Sports Illustrated* carried an article on team chemistry. It contrasted the success of athletic squads which have it with the failure of those which don't. An example cited of the latter was the 1993-94 North Carolina Tar

Heels basketball team. Returning every starter but one from their '93 national championship, plus the best recruiting class in the country, the Heels seemed a cinch for another trophy. Instead they failed even to make the Final Four. Why? The hotshot recruits threatened the status of some veteran players, who responded by giving the freshmen the cold shoulder on and off the court. The result: a divided and unhealthy team that fizzled when it should have sizzled.

If the Church ever gets its chemistry right, if it ever realizes what a fantastic team it has, if it ever quits fighting itself and unitedly confronts the opposition, the devil's agenda will be in big trouble. So often he blinds Christians to our identity and potential. Stops us from recognizing and wielding our true power. Keeps us divided and demoralized. Leaves us unaware that he, not each other, is whom we should be fighting.

God wants us to know who the real enemy is, and how he operates.

A Villainous Clone

Satan had already been part of the kingdom of God. He knew how a kingdom runs. Since he's not a creator but an imitator, his tactics are to mimic, co-opt, pervert, distort, or misuse the ways of God. The archenemy's kingdom is nothing new. It mirrors (albeit, with a cracked mirror) the one from which he was expelled.

With this in mind Paul gives the Ephesians this pep talk (6:10-12): "Finally, be strong in the Lord and in his mighty power. Put on the full armor of God so that you can take your stand against the devil's schemes. For our struggle is not against flesh and blood, but against the rulers, against the authorities, against the powers of this dark world and against the spiritual forces of evil in the heavenly realms."

In simple form the apostle outlines Satan's kingdom. These tremendously important words remind us that Christians are at war, and not against flesh and blood. We're not battling other human beings, not other Christians, not even sinners. We're squared off against unseen forces of evil.

"We wrestle ...." In the Roman world wrestling was nothing like the charades shown today on TV. It was grim business. Sometimes the loser even had his eyes gouged out. Paul was picturing intense hand-to-hand combat. Such is spiritual warfare: a desperate, high-stakes, very-close-and-personal brawl. It's an often lonely, one-on-one bout with the enemy of our souls. (Though we must remember we're not actually grappling solo. We're part of a tag team: God wrestles alongside us. As Paul cheers us on in Romans 8:31, "If God is for us, who can be against us?")

"... Not against flesh and blood." Every believer should eliminate from his/her mind the thought that people are the enemy. Yes, it seems that way at times, even with other Christians. You feel that, if the sinners don't get the best of you, the saints will. Yet even when the devil uses people as his tools, seldom do they realize what's happening.

It's amazing how often pastors, deacons, church members, and dedicated Christians are used by the devil to harm one another—like that dog and cat—without realizing it. Like the Midianites when Gideon's three hundred surprised them in the darkness, we tear into each other rather than the true attacker. Many churches have been neutralized, their kingdom potential squandered, by this kind of spiritual espionage.

Church members aren't the opposition. The pastor isn't. The board isn't. The deacons aren't. Even the worst unbeliever isn't. Satan is. The devil gets by with murder when God's soldiers shoot at the wrong targets. Nothing delights the deceiver more than the feuding faithful.

An X-Ray of Darkness

"We wrestle not against flesh and blood, but ..." Ponder the language in various translations of the remainder of Paul's sentence. We wrestle against ...

principalities
evil rulers of the unseen world
organizations and powers that are spiritual
wicked spiritual forces
the rulers
the sovereignties
rulers of the darkness of this world
mighty satanic beings and great evil princes of darkness
 who rule the world
the unseen power that controls this dark world
the world rulers of this present darkness
cosmic powers of this dark age
the authorities and potentates of this dark world
huge numbers of wicked spirits in the spirit world
spirit agents from the very headquarters of evil
spiritual hosts of wickedness
superhuman forces of evil in the heavens

Paul is trying to impress upon his readers that a vast host of spiritual enemies is aligned against them. Since they're spiritual, they're unseen. Since they're spiritual, they can only be spiritually discerned. The vast majority of human beings remains clueless to this legion's existence. But Christians needn't be clueless.

The unseen spiritual forces of evil are probably so huge that when believers gather to worship, more invisible spirits show up than visible worshipers. Each of us must have one and perhaps more especially assigned to him/her. That doesn't mean you should panic. He who is within you is greater than he that is in the world. Even if Satan sent in a dozen battalions of demons against one Christian, that one *in Christ* more than levels the playing field. We shouldn't be scared, but we should be aware.

Once you understand the cosmic powers waging war all around you, you're not in a fog. You know what's going on. Like a football team that has thoroughly scouted its opponent, you understand what you're up against, what tricks and tendencies to watch for, what strengths and weaknesses you face, and what strategies will lead to victory.

Paul's list depicts an organized force. Of course we know heaven's army is highly organized, though the Bible gives sparse details. It does mention cherubim and seraphim, archangels and ministering spirits. Apparently Lucifer, before his fall, served as vice regent of the celestial realm. When God court-martialed him, he evidently structured his kingdom of darkness along hierarchical lines similar to what he'd known.

Compare the language in Ephesians 1:21 (Christ is "far above all rule and authority, power and dominion") with 6:12 (we struggle "against the rulers, against the authorities, against the powers of this dark world and against the spiritual forces of evil in the heavenly realms"). The same organizational terminology is applied to the forces of heaven and of hell. Thus Satan mimics the kingdom of God, with all of his battalions (chief angels, princes, world rulers, etc.) operating under his command.

Satan is a *person*. The moment we forget that and think of him as just an influence (like some people view the Holy Spirit), we're in trouble. Evil is not some vague, impersonal force infiltrating the earth that cannot be accurately pinned down. The Bible refutes that from cover to cover. Most telling of all, the wilderness temptations of Jesus unmask the individual, personal nature of His tempter: God incarnate squared off against godlessness personified.

A Criminal's Aliases

One of the best ways to learn the nature of God is to study his names. Ditto the dean of darkness. Here are some of his titles:

1) ***Dragon*** (Revelation 12:7-9)—"There was war in heaven. Michael and his angels fought against the dragon, and the dragon and his angels fought back. But he was not strong enough, and they lost their place in heaven. The great dragon was hurled down—that ancient serpent called the devil or Satan, who leads the whole world astray. He was hurled to the earth, and his angels with him." Probably an alternate form of *derkomai* (to look), the word pictures a fabulous creature, a fascinating kind of serpent that could hold onlookers spellbound.

2) ***Ancient Serpent*** (Revelation 12:9)—*archaios* (old or primeval). *Serpent* connotes sharpness of vision and cunning. Originally the serpent was one of God's highest creations, and it became the instrument through which Satan scammed Adam and Eve. The devil is a sly, wily, sinister character. And he's been around since ancient times. We're not weighing in against a rookie. He knows all the holds and every trick.

3) ***Devil*** (John 8:44)—"You belong to your father, the devil, and you want to carry out your father's desire. He was a murderer from the beginning, not holding to the truth, for there is no truth in him. When he lies, he speaks his native language, for he is a liar and the father of lies." The devil (*diabolos*) is completely evil, a diabolical slanderer and false accuser. He distorts and discredits the truth at every opportunity.

4) ***Satan*** (Revelation 12:10)—*the accuser*. "Then I heard a loud voice in heaven say: 'Now have come the salvation and

the power and the kingdom of our God, and the authority of his Christ. For the accuser of our brothers, who accuses them before our God day and night, has been hurled down.'" Those who engage in the "ministry of accusation" are assisting Satan in his work.

5) ***Deceiver*** (Genesis 3:13; Revelation 20:10). *Planao* means "to cause to roam or wander." He tricks people into wandering from the path of safety, truth, or virtue. He's constantly putting up detours that redirect toward disaster those who aren't heeding God's road map.

6) ***Prince***. Since being cast out of heaven, the archfiend no longer is a prince of God. Now he rules as the "prince of demons" (Matthew 12:24). As the "prince of the power of the air" (Ephesians 2:2). As the "prince of this world" (John 14:30).

7) ***Murderer*** (John 8:44). He exists only to "steal and kill and destroy" (John 10:10). If only those who purchase his poisonous products recognized that. If people really knew the devil, they wouldn't want to have anything to do with him.

8) ***Liar*** (John 8:44). He never, ever tells the truth (though he twists the facts and peddles half-truths). He's like an auctioneer in Oklahoma City who always begins by warning the crowd, "From now on, don't believe a thing I say." Then he tells a few jokes, disarms the audience with folksy warmth, and sells them a bunch of junk. To hear him working, you'd think you were bidding for solid gold treasures. His listeners have willingly forgotten his disclaimer. Likewise people ignore the Bible's warning—"don't believe a thing Satan says"—and succumb to his charming falsehoods, which he rattles off with the tongue-teasing ease of an auctioneer.

9) ***Abaddon, Apollyon*** (Revelation 9:11). Those are the Hebrew and Greek names for *destroyer*. What better name could be given to one who is the "angel of the Abyss"?

10) ***Beelzebub*** (Matthew 12:24). He is the "dung god." Now that's truth in advertising.

11) ***Belial*** (2 Corinthians 6:15)—worthless, of no account.

12) ***The evil one*** (Matthew 6:13). The more accurate version of the Lord's Prayer is "... and lead us not into temptation, but deliver us from *the evil one*." Our enemy is a person, not merely a principle.

Hell on the Flow Chart

This, then, is the profile of the CEO of hell's hierarchy. What does the organization itself look like? It includes these ranks or levels:

1) ***Principalities*** (*arche, archoi*)—chief in various orders, ranks, and place; or "cosmic powers" (NEB), universal in their impact.

2) ***Powers*** (*exousias*)—the same word used of the Holy Spirit: authority, delegated influence. Don't attribute to Satan that which God alone can do. The devil is not omnipresent. You may never have encountered him directly. He delegates authority to his demonic underlings throughout the earth. He met Jesus personally, and he entered into Judas to orchestrate the Master's betrayal. But he depends on his villainous hordes to multiply his influence.

3) ***Rulers*** or ***world rulers*** (*kosmokrator*)—those who aspire to world control. "We are up against the unseen power that controls this dark world" (Ephesians 6:12, *Phillips*), "against the Sovereignties and the Powers that originate the darkness in this world" (JB). These are highly organized great powers, evil angels who seek to control the hearts of those in authoritative positions in the world, to prevent these movers and shakers from submitting themselves to the truth and power of God.

Satan often appears smarter than the Church. He goes after men and women of influence to maximize his impact.

(How important it is, therefore, as part of strategic spiritual warfare that we bombard with prayer government leaders and other powerful persons.)

4) ***Spiritual forces of wickedness*** (*ta pneumatika tes poner-ias*)—These forces are spiritual, not physical. They are overwhelmingly evil: vile and fiendish (the same word is used in Ephesians 6:13, "when the day of *evil* comes"). *Poneria* was used to describe rotten meat, a constant concern in the ancient world. No wonder the Bible so often calls demons unclean. The legions of evil are rancid and rotten to the core, and they yearn to turn every person God created into a stench-filled, putrefying spirit. Even the decay of the physical body betrays sin's gangrenous infection of the universe.

Christian Counter-Espionage

The old serpent's organization pursues the primary goal of wrecking God's kingdom. And its strategy includes a game plan for derailing every sincere follower of God. Satan's minions carry a scouting report and scheme for you. Therefore you need to stay on your spiritual toes (and knees).

Each person has strengths and vulnerabilities. Certain temptations have never worked on me. For instance, I've never been tempted to abuse alcohol. I saw early on what fools people became when they got drunk. (I can make a big enough fool of myself without liquor's help.) Patience, however, is a different story. The patience pears on my Fruit of the Spirit tree to this day remain small and scarce. The enemy of my soul can exploit me much more easily there. So with each of us: our temptations are tailored to our vulnerabilities.

Not only that, but the more effective in God's service you become, the more you'll be targeted. We should be saddened but not shocked when influential and visible Christian leaders experience moral failure. Though such roles may seem glamorous, they're really dangerous, for they lie directly in the sights of hell's snipers.

A key, therefore, to avoiding disaster is identifying the evil empire and its tactics. An organization like the CIA constantly watches for traitors and impostors among its ranks, knowing an undetected double agent can imperil lives and the security of the nation. God's holy nation should remain similarly alert. "Be self-controlled and vigilant always," Peter warns (1 Peter 5:8, *Phillips*), "because your enemy the devil is always about," like a lion ready to devour its prey.

Jesus loved Simon Peter just as much that pivotal day in Caesarea Philippi as he ever had, but when He spied the devil's hand in the disciple's well-meaning rebuke, he responded sternly. "Get behind me, Satan! You are a stumbling block to me; you do not have in mind the things of God, but the things of men" (Matthew 16:23). Sounding so innocent and sensible, Simon's words were the diabolical one's tool to divert the Messiah from His mission. And they came from the lips of one who'd just exclaimed, "You are the Christ, the Son of the Living God." That's an eye-popping reminder that any of us at any moment is capable of being the deceiver's dupe.

"Know the enemy so well," God warns, "that you can recognize his tactics anytime, anywhere.

As Eugene Peterson paraphrases Paul (*The Message*):

> God is strong, and he wants you strong. So take everything the Master has set out for you, well-made weapons of the best materials. And put them to use so you will be able to stand up to everything the Devil throws your way. This is no afternoon athletic contest that we'll walk away from and forget about in a couple of hours. This is for keeps, a life-or-death fight to the

finish against the Devil and all his angels.

Be prepared. You're up against far more than you can handle on your own. Take all the help you can get, every weapon God has issued, so that when it's all over but the shouting you'll still be on your feet.

The devil is a dragon. A serpent. A liar and slanderer and deceiver and accuser. He's a spiritual slime ball whose one purpose is to ruin your life. Don't underestimate his malevolence.

In *A View from the Zoo* (Word, 1987), former zoo keeper Gary Richmond writes about the glandular change raccoons go through at about two years of age. When that happens, he explains, a pet raccoon is likely to attack its master. That's seriously bad news, since a 30-pound coon can seem like a 100-pound dog in a fight. However, Richmond's friend Julie was undeterred. "It will be different for me," she assured with a smile. "Bandit wouldn't hurt me. He just wouldn't."

Three months later Julie underwent plastic surgery on her face. "For no apparent reason" her cuddly pet had turned on her.

Whatever alias Satan operates under, however innocuous his approach to you seems, don't be fooled. He's lying, cheating, poisonous, murderous scum. If you don't recognize and remain alert to the reality of his evil kingdom, he'll maul you when you're least expecting it.

Be God's good scout. Be prepared.

You may be the heavyweight champion of the world,
You might be a socialite with a long string of pearls,
You may be a businessman or some high-degree thief,
They may call you doctor or they may call you chief,
But you're gonna have to serve somebody,
You're gonna have to serve somebody.
Now it may be the devil, or it may be the Lord,
But you're gonna have to serve somebody.

—Bob Dylan

The world is poor because her fortune is buried in the sky and all her treasure maps are of the earth.

—Calvin Miller

5

Hell's Triple Threat

A couple of decades ago one of the toughest offenses to defend in college football was the triple option. Talented teams rode that play to tremendous success, none more so than the Oklahoma Sooners and their "wishbone" attack. On almost every play the opposing defense had to defend against three threats simultaneously. The quarterback could hand the ball to the fullback crashing through the middle, or keep it himself as he danced along the line of scrimmage and headed up field, or pitch to the trailing halfback. Not knowing whether the quarterback had the ball or was giving it to one of the other two kept defenses frozen just long enough to create many big gains.

Satan is a triple threat quarterback, his effectiveness increased by the two teammates running with him. The world, the flesh, and the devil: from its launching, the Church has had to line up nose-to-nose against these three.

The "world" refers neither to the planet we live on nor its inhabitants. It means the fallen, godless world system. Christians, especially the very conservative, often misperceive (to the evil one's delight) worldliness as certain external, cultural trappings. The Bible, however, sees worldliness as an internal disease, a mindset that opposes God and promotes self.

Nor does "flesh" in this context refer to the physical body but to human nature divorced from God. It's the name for that independent weed that, left unchecked, overwhelms the garden of the heart and chokes out Christ's Lordship. If flesh had a theme song, it would be "I Did It My Way."

In reality, Satan hardly needs to carry the ball himself against unbelievers. They are already outmatched (2 Corinthians 4:4) against the flesh and the world. He can just hand the ball off to his backfield mates and watch them overrun lost people.

As the prince of this world, he already has it organized to suppress the truth and keep people from the knowledge of the gospel. He uses an educational system rife with anti-Christian agendas; an entertainment industry which relentlessly erodes biblical and moral values; a media which distorts and downplays Christian truth; and business and government's worship of the false gods of power and money.

That's not to insinuate there are no godly people in these areas, or that all unbelievers are in conscious conspiracy—often they have no idea they're the serpent's pawns. Nevertheless this pagan world (*kosmos*) is orchestrated by the deceiver.

Harold Lindsell writes (*The World, the Flesh, and the Devil*, Canon Press, 1973):

> Wherever there is mischief afoot, Satan is sure to be involved. He is the one who precipitates wars, encourages men in their lusts, causes men to question the Word of God, and tells men they can play with sin and win. He stands by every drunkard's side. He peers out of the window of every house of prostitution. He watches over the shoulder of every thief. He feeds words into the mouth of every blasphemer. He controls the mind and thoughts of every pornographer. He sits beside the statesmen in the chancelleries of the world as they decide the destiny of nations.

Believers, however, struggling against the flesh and the world, are special targets of Satan. Though we are more aware of the spiritual dangers around us, we are not immune to them. This fallen world system contains traps for even the most dedicated disciple.

As the World Turns

It's critical that we understand what worldliness is. And what it isn't. For example, one of the most surprising and insightful uses of the word *world* is found in 1 Peter 3:3, 4, where it's translated "adornment." This oft-used—and abused—text says, "Your beauty should not come from outward adornment, such as braided hair and the wearing of gold jewelry and fine clothes. Instead, it should be that of your inner self, the unfading beauty of a gentle and quiet spirit, which is of great worth in God's sight."

Donald Grey Barnhouse translates these two verses like this: "Whose world, let it not be the world of the beauty shop, the jeweler or the dress maker, but let it be the hidden man of the heart, in that which is not corruptible, even the world of the meek and quiet spirit, which is in the sight of God of great price" (*The Invisible War*, Zondervan Publishing House, Grand Rapids, 1965).

The Living Bible paraphrases the passage: "Don't be concerned about the outward beauty that depends on jewelry, or beautiful clothes, or hair arrangement. Be beautiful inside, in your hearts, with the lasting charm of a gentle and quiet spirit that is so precious to God."

Understood correctly, this passage opens our eyes to the true nature of worldliness. Despite preaching you may have heard to the contrary, these verses have nothing to do with whether a woman fixes her hair or wears jewelry and attractive clothing.

Such preaching was especially humorous because of the way the King James text was worded: " ... of plaiting of hair, and of wearing of gold, or of putting on of apparel." If fancy hairdos and jewelry were taboo, why not forbid women to wear clothes also, as the verse plainly said?

Don't you know that Lucifer loves to get us sidetracked with such trivial nonsense? Then he kills two birds with the same rock. Christianity becomes so weird and unappealing that people who need the living water are turned off. And Christians get so caught up in legalistic minutiae that we don't even notice when real worldliness has infected us.

The Heart of the Matter

Peter's words have absolutely nothing to do with whether a woman should wear earrings or visit the beauty salon. Ladies, fix yourself up all you want. Just don't let that become your world, the passage is saying. Don't live for external appearance or allow those interests to shape your value system. Treasure instead those beauty aids for the spirit and put most of your energy into fixing yourself up on the inside. Beauty may be only skin deep, but worldliness goes all the way to the heart.

The Oxford English Dictionary defines cosmos as "worldly affairs; the aggregate of things earthly; the whole circle of earthly goods, endowments, riches, advantages, pleasures, etc., which, although hollow and frail and fleeting, stir desire, seduce from God, and are obstacles to the cause of Christ." Could a book of theology have put it more clearly? The Christian constantly battles the lure of things and experiences and achievements which, while temporary, threaten to block the sunlight of the eternal.

With that threat in mind, John cautions us in his first epistle, "Do not love the world or anything in the world. If anyone loves the world, the love of the Father is not in him. For everything in the world—the cravings of sinful man, the lust of his eyes and the boasting of what he has and does—comes not from the Father but from the world. *The world and its desires pass away*, but the man who does the will of God lives forever" (1 John 2:15-17, italics added).

John isn't advocating we refuse to do business with the banks or drop out of society. He's not telling us not to be into the world but to guard against the world being in us. John is pleading for us not to fall in love with this fallen world and its ways of thinking and living. For it's temporary. It will pass away.

In *Growing Deep in the Christian Life* (Multnomah, 1986), Chuck Swindoll relates a story that Charlie "Tremendous" Jones tells on himself. The irrepressible Jones walked down into his basement to assess the damage following the devastating Youngstown flood. He found waist-high mud and gunk in the room where he displayed all his trophies and plaques. "I stood there staring in disbelief," Jones recalls. "Then I heard God say, 'Charlie Not-So-Tremendous Jones, don't worry about all this. I was gonna burn it all up anyway.'"

Don't love position or possessions or pleasure. Where your treasure lies, Jesus noted, your heart will be also. And if your treasure's stored in the wrong vault, it will rust or rot or disappear. Fame is fleeting. Things wear out. Pleasure loses its lure. Seeking fulfillment down those alleyways is like gulping salt water. The more you drink, the thirstier you grow; and if you ingest enough, it will kill you. Only Christ's living water satisfies on and on. Only the one who does the will of God will weather the ages.

How then should the believer deal with the enticements of worldliness? What tactic do you and I use? The key word is *follow*. "Pursue righteousness, godliness, faith, love, endurance and gentleness," directs 1 Timothy 6:11. Aim for them, set your heart on them, chase after them like a dog runs a rabbit. Just as your best strategy to avoid extra-marital temptations is to pursue intimacy with your spouse, so you best escape the world's tentacles when you're running hard into the arms of Jesus. Spiritual passion is a marvelous antidote for carnal obsession.

A couple in love has eyes only for each other. They are drawn together like magnets. You can't keep them apart. Likewise one who's fallen in love with Jesus loses the yen for competing attractions.

"Seek first his kingdom and his righteousness," Jesus taught, "and all these things will be given to you as well" (Matthew 6:33). Hold on to God tenaciously and everything else loosely. Adore Him with all your mental and physical and spiritual capacity. As David moans from the desert, "O God, you are my God, earnestly I seek you; my soul thirsts for you, my body longs for you, in a dry and weary land where there is no water ... your love is better than life" (Psalm 63:1, 3).

Flesh Feud

The Bible doesn't mince words regarding the flesh either. It is at war with the Spirit, and vice versa, insists Galatians 5:17. Remember that the flesh we're talking about is human nature unleashed from God's grace and control. Consider it dangerous and destructive, like a runaway car with no driver.

Two opposite errors can be made in this area. One is to assume that Christians are forever under the thumb of fleshly impulses. Romans 7:15 is seen as normative spirituality—"I do not understand what I do. For what I want to do I do not do, but what I hate I do." The emphasis of salvation falls predominantly on imputed righteousness and very little on imparted righteousness. God has declared us "not guilty," and we're on our way to heaven, but we have little to show for it in terms of Christlikeness and spiritual victory.

The other extreme is to claim for oneself a semi-glorified state. Some folks can't ever admit to sinning. They act as though they're impervious even to temptation. They walk around with an air of invincibility. In their reasoning, sanctification has chased the flesh completely out of the county. They never get angry; they get righteously indignant. They're not stubborn; they're determined. They don't commit sins; they make mistakes (and precious few of those).

The first error sentences sincere persons to trifling lives of guilt and frustration, dwelling as paupers right outside the open gates of the King's castle. The second error creates super-spiritual Pharisees and sets them up for a devastating fall. No one makes a more inviting target for the enemy than those who are confident they can't become targets.

The truth lies in between, doesn't it? Once again listen to Harold Lindsell's words (*The World, the Flesh, and the Devil*, Canon Press, 1973): "The Christian is a redeemed man who is called to serve the Redeemer. But he lives in a world shaped by conflict and is engaged in a life and death struggle ... It is a warfare that does not cease until death, but it is also a life of challenge and filled with glorious possibilities."

What tactic do we use against the flesh? The key word here is *flee*. Again, 1 Timothy 6:11 warns the man of God to "flee from all this." Flee what? Flee the evil desires of youth (2 Timothy 2:22). Flee sexual immorality (1 Corinthians 6:18). Flee sinful desires which war against the soul (1 Peter 2:11). "Flee" is the flip side of the "pursue" coin. We are to run just as hard from the flesh as we are to chase after godliness.

Use the same technique toward the flesh as the radio disk jockey prescribed for seasickness. "Get up early in the morning," he advised, "and eat a large breakfast of fried eggs, pork rinds, and molasses. Then head down to the dock early. Stand on the pier and, extending your right arm high above your head, move your hand rhythmically from side to side. Continue this for some time, until your boat has disappeared from view, at which time you can stop waving and go back home."

Some problems are handled better from a distance. Be warned. It doesn't matter who you are, how much religion you have, or how important a position you hold in the church. There are times when you'd better grab your coat and run. If you think you're so spiritual you can flirt with temptation and not get nailed, you're already halfway to disaster. Being a Christian doesn't inoculate you to desire.

Once I preached a revival at a church where the secretary-treasurer had locked her radar on the pastor. It was obvious. So was the fact that the pastor was enjoying it. I don't think he had any thought of starting an affair, but he was lapping up the attention she showered on him. Two or three nights into the services, I pulled him aside and spoke bluntly. "Mister, when you see that woman coming, you'd better run, run, run." He laughed at me, because he was sure he could handle it. A few months later the sad truth of his becoming a victim of the flesh surfaced.

Another pastor, after committing sexual indiscretion, sat across the table from me one day and pleaded for me to tell other ministers what he'd found out the hard way, that "it's impossible to climb so high that you cannot fall." Each person must recognize his/her limits. Because you are "fearfully and wonderfully made," you should respect your awesome potential for good or evil and "continue to work out your salvation with fear and trembling" (Philippians 2:12). If you never tremble, then you're not regarding the dangers of the flesh seriously enough.

God will alert you when danger is on the horizon, if you'll stay tuned. Once when I was pastoring, I attempted to visit a church family. When I arrived, no one was at home except the wife's sister who had been staying with them. She greeted me with a warm smile and welcomed me in. But no sooner had the door closed behind me than a voice within my spirit whispered, "You'd better leave." I excused myself, explaining that I had things to do and would return when the others were at home. Within a year I found out that she had had close encounters of the illicit kind with a number of men and was now pregnant.

Sometimes the bravest thing a believer can do is run away.

Tackling the Devil

We face hell's triple option: the world, the flesh, ... and the devil. The biblical tactic with him is to *fight*. Once more from 1 Timothy 6, "Fight the good fight of the faith" (v. 12). We're never told to run from the evil one. In Ephesians 6 the key word is "stand," a military term meaning, "Hold your ground and don't give an inch." In 1 Peter 5:8, 9 where the enemy is described as a roaring lion on the prowl, the orders are similar. "Be self-controlled and alert ... Resist him, standing firm in the faith."

We're told to stand and fight because Lucifer is already a defeated foe, and God has issued us the weapons needed to engage him. Our Commander in Chief will "restore you and make you strong, firm and steadfast. To him be the power for ever and ever" (5:10, 11). We win by *submitting* and *resisting*. By obeying God and opposing Satan.

Follow godliness. Flee the flesh. Fight the dragon. That's a three-pronged winning strategy.

During the glory days of the wishbone offense, it often seemed unstoppable. Television analysts, however, would remind viewers of its limitations. One way to slow it down was to stop the quarterback. His quickness, reads of the defense, and deception was what made the triple option whir. To handle him was to break the 'bone.

Another key was to build a lead. The wishbone offense, designed to run the ball most of the time and use the pass as a surprise, was not a good catch-up formation. It wasn't tailored to come from behind late in the game.

So it is with hell's triple threat. Our battle is not primarily with the world and flesh but the devil. He is the author of sin, the quarterback that keeps it all going. And his game plan is to overwhelm us. Put him two or three touchdowns behind, remove the element of surprise from his play book, and the prince of darkness is doomed to defeat. That's just what Jesus Christ did. He surprised the deceiver and put him in a hole as deep as the pits of hell.

Have you checked the scoreboard recently? It says that we're winning.

The devil is the top hidden persuader—the master of subliminal motivation.

—*Jess C. Moody*

Temptation is Satan's opening wedge into a man's being. He does not want to stop there. If a man will obey demonic promptings to do evil, Satan will do worse with him by far than merely to tempt him.

—*McCandlish Phillips*

The devil is easy to identify. He appears when you're terribly tired and makes a very reasonable request which you know you shouldn't grant.

— *Fiorello La Guardia*

6

Satanic Strategies

Before Western Union began including punctuation marks in all their telegrams, a customer lost a mint of money over a missing period. His wife wanted to purchase a $75,000 necklace. When she telegraphed her husband for permission, he responded, "No. Price too high." At least he thought he did.

The telegram that arrived at her door, however, seemed to say with romantic flair, "No price too high."

That kind of garbled message happens with sin also. When the tempter entices us with forbidden activities or relationships or possessions, God's Word firmly speaks, "No! The price is too great." However, when we want to do something wrong badly enough, we willingly yield to Satan's distortion of truth. "No price is too great if I really want this, or if it satisfies me, or if ...."

The cost of sin is always too high. Period!

Spiritual warfare is no genteel pursuit. It's not a hobby you pursue on your day off, like a round of golf. It's a no-holds-barred fight to the finish.

The Bible delivers sobering news. If you believe in Jesus Christ, you're already at war. This combat has no civilian bystanders. If you don't realize that, you're in great jeopardy. As dangerous as a battlefield is for the soldier, it's ten times worse for the person who strolls into the line of fire oblivious to what's transpiring.

We'd better be alert and armed, God's Word warns, because the stakes are very high. "Be strong in the Lord and in his mighty power. Put on the full armor of God so that you can take your stand against the devil's schemes. For our struggle is not against flesh and blood but against the rulers, against the authorities, against the powers of this dark world, against the spiritual forces of evil in the heavenly realms" (Ephesians 6:10-12).

That's strong talk. The apostle stresses not only the celestial nature of this war but the strength of the opposition. We must fully prepare "in order that Satan might not outwit us. For we are not unaware of his schemes" (2 Corinthians 2:11). Or, "to keep Satan from gaining the advantage over us; for we are not ignorant of his designs" (RSV). Or, "Satan must not be allowed to get the better of us; we know his wiles all too well" (NEB).

A Thousand Faces

Note these key words: *Schemes* or *wiles* (Ephesians 6:11) translates *methodeia*, which includes the idea of method, especially a deceptive or shady practice. It describes the tricks of the con artist and swindler. *Designs* or *devices* (2 Corinthians 2:11) comes from *noema*, which means something that is arranged or contrived to bring about a particular result. These are ingenious or clever traps to trick one's victims into doing what they do not want to do.

Satan is the master of disguise. He's better than any movie makeup artist. Like horror film legend Lon Chaney, the deceiver is a "man of a thousand faces." Perhaps to the other names the devil has been given we should add "chameleon."

As song lyrics by Stormie Omartian ("Alive and Well," *Adam Again*, Myrrh Records, 1976) picture him:

> I'm alive and well and I'm living in L.A.
> Or in anyone's heart who wants to listen to my ways.
> Got a million faces I want to let you see;
> You can share in all I have if you open up to me.
>
> I'm alive and well and I'm living in L.A.
> Or in anyone's heart who wants to listen to my ways.
> If you want to think I wear a red suit, that's fine,
> But the truth is I wear whatever suits me at the time.

The prince of sinners hides a pack of tricks up his sleeve. Like a raging lion, he can make a frontal assault to scare the daylights out of you (1 Peter 5:8). Or he can appear as an angel of light, offering friendly advice (2 Corinthians 11:14); he knows that bit well from his pre-fall days. He plays a wealth of other roles as well, and he's great at picking the right one for the person and the moment. Like a veteran boxer, Satan searches out his opponent's weaknesses until he finds the best spot to exploit.

Eve of Destruction

Zoom in for a closer look at some of the strategies he used with biblical targets. In one instance he acts as a slanderer. In another he plays the accuser. In yet other encounters he takes on the part of tempter or sifter. Don't let the ancient settings of these stories mislead you, for the techniques are as universal and contemporary as Madison Avenue (whose methods bear a striking resemblance to the great impostor's).

The first encounter humanity ever had with Satan is recounted in the third chapter of Genesis:

> Now the serpent was more crafty than any of the wild animals the Lord God had made. He said to the woman, "Did God really say, 'You must not eat from any tree in the garden?'"
>
> The woman said to the serpent, "We may eat fruit from the trees in the garden, but God did say, 'You must not eat fruit from the tree that is in the middle of the garden, and you must not touch it, or you will die.'"
>
> "You will not surely die," the serpent said to the woman. "For God knows that when you eat of it, your eyes will be opened, and you will be like God, knowing good and evil."
>
> When the woman saw that the fruit of the tree was good for food and pleasing to the eye, and also desirable for gaining wisdom, she took some and ate. She also gave some to her husband, who was with her, and he ate it. Then the eyes of both of them were opened, and they realized they were naked; so they sewed fig

leaves together and made coverings for themselves (Genesis 3:1-7).

"Has God said ...?" In this simple but sinister query lies one of the great secrets of Satan's success. He's wise enough not to deny up front God's authority when dealing with believers. Instead he sows the insidious seed of suspicion. What if God cannot be trusted? What if He's holding out on us? What if He doesn't have our best interests in mind after all?

Eve is hooked. She's become emotionally involved in the sideways challenge to God's integrity. In her response she adds to God's instructions: "and you must not touch it." God hadn't said anything about touching. In Eve's mind the Creator's "unreasonable" restrictions are being painted in more severe tones than they had been given.

Adding to and distorting God's Word is a common sin. We Bible-believing Christians rail against liberals who tear apart and subtract from the Word. However, we are also guilty at times of muddying and polluting the stream of truth with the debris we toss into it. Like the toxic wastes of legalism. And the Spirit-clogging debris of tradition. And the chemical spills of extra-biblical nonsense. And the seepage of political and cultural fads. And the trash of Scripture-twisting to suit our biases. Sometimes we reduce the living, liberating water of the gospel to a noxious trickle. How many would-be believers have remained thirsty and marooned in sin's desert because the water we offered wasn't fit to drink?

That Three-letter Word

Once Eve had taken the bait, the slanderer reeled her in. He slipped from questioning God's Word to denying it. Having undermined the Most High's credibility, he markets his own. "You will not surely die," he scoffs those same words he's repeated a billion times since. "No price is too high. Go ahead and flout God's boundaries; there are no negative consequences. Who told you that nonsense anyway, some fuddy-duddy deity?"

It's no more popular to mention *sin* in today's culture than in Edenville. Listen to the big shots who get caught. They tell us they "made mistakes." They "used poor judgment." Their actions are "regrettable." But they never use the "s" word.

How intriguing that Karl Menninger, writing not from a Christian but a clinical perspective, posed his famous question: "Whatever Became of Sin?" and concluded his book by calling on preachers to deal with the subject once again, to proclaim repentance and God's forgiveness. His call represents a cry in the wilderness of secular morality.

CBS and ABC and CNN don't want to talk about sin. They'll cut people off who bring up the topic. I was both surprised and proud at Dan and Marilyn Quayle's courageous responses during a Barbara Walters interview a few years ago, especially in light of all the abuse they had taken in the press. "I understand," Walters posed to him, "that you are a born-again Christian."

"Yes," he replied, "the greatest thing that ever happened to me was when I met Jesus Christ."

Walters probed further. "I understand that you pray."

"Yes, we pray every day. That's one of the greatest privileges of a Christian."

Those were courageous words you seldom hear in the public square. The pagan world doesn't want to discuss God and morality and sin. It's big into *tolerance* these days (of everything but Christianity, it seems). But the Bible says that the soul which sins will die (Ezekiel 18:4). If we violate the Most High's laws, we will suffer and we will cause other people to suffer. To think otherwise is to swallow a vintage lie from the winery of hell.

Aw, adultery's okay, Satan reassures. *Homosexuality's okay. Promiscuity and greed and selfish indulgence are risk-free. Trust me*, he soothes us in his best salesman's voice, *I'm the expert in the field.*

Isn't it curious how scientifically-minded folks who respect God's physical laws flout His moral laws. They know that to step off the roof of the Empire State building would bring certain death. Yet they leap from a skyscraper-high pile of sinful choices and think they will float harmlessly to the ground. "Eve, honey, do what you want," purred the prince of propaganda. "You won't get hurt." Then he proceeded to sell her a nice piece of paradise-turned-swampland.

From questioning God's authority the serpent turned to questioning His love. "Does the Creator really want what's best for you? Why, He knows that when you eat of that fruit, you will become as godlike as He is" (the same grandiosity Lucifer himself had fallen for). "He doesn't want you to become all you can be."

Satan is a slanderer. That's his first stratagem. He slanders God. He questions the King's authority, besmirches His reputation, and impugns His motives. When a person buys the liar's lines, that individual stands one step away from outright rebellion.

A Prosecuting Attorney

The next classic contest occurs in the book of Job, and admittedly some aspects of this strange scenario are hard to fathom. One day the sons of God presented themselves before Jehovah, and Satan also showed up for their get-together (he's quite a mixer, isn't he?). When God broached the subject of His stellar servant, the accuser countered with a prosecutorial opening statement.

"Have you considered my servant Job?" God began. "There is no one on earth like him; he is blameless and upright, a man who fears God and shuns evil."

The devil responded something like this: "Yeah, yeah, I've heard of him, but if You think he loves You so much, You're greatly mistaken. Let me tell You what's really going on with that guy. The only reason he serves You is because You keep a bullet-proof shield around him; and I can't get at him. Why, You prosper everything he does—no wonder he jumps at Your command. Just take away his cushy circumstances and he'll scream curses at You."

Well, God did and Job didn't. So the dung god showed up again. "Have you considered my servant Job?" God Almighty exults.

"It's still not a fair fight," growled the enemy. "You've let me destroy all he has, but You won't let me lay a finger on the man himself. Give me carte blanche and just watch how quickly he reaches the breaking point."

"All right," agreed Jehovah. "Do anything you want with Job except kill him. I will not completely remove My hedge of protection around him, but you can take your best shot."

Now Job didn't know about these conversations until much later. The poor guy probably wondered what had caused the bottom to fall out of his world. He didn't comprehend what was taking place, and that made his dark night of the soul that much blacker. However, God knew what was going down. He was putting His servant on display. He was turning the spotlight full-tilt on Job to say, "Look, world; look, hosts of heaven. Here's a man whose commitment is unconditional. Nothing can turn him."

The devil chronically accuses God's people. Always has. He questions their commitment and badmouths their character. Many fall for it. The church is full of pastors and laypersons who live beneath the ever-ominous clouds of condemnation. Who pull around a wagon load of guilt. Whose shoulders bear the leaden shroud of spiritual inadequacy. Most condemnation comes from Satan, not from heaven. "For God did not send his Son into the world to condemn the world, but to save the world through him" (John 3:17).

Lucifer also has helpers in the Church, such as ministers who revel in leveling their listeners, and Church members who circle like sharks searching for fresh blood. Nothing will cripple a group of believers sooner than a critical, condemning atmosphere.

The gospel, on the other hand, is good news. It doesn't enslave souls. It sets them free. "Who will bring any charge against those whom God has chosen? It is God who justifies. Who is he that condemns? Christ Jesus, who died—more than that, who was raised to life—is at the right hand of God and is also interceding for us" (Romans 8:33, 34).

It doesn't matter who's prosecuting you when the Lord is your defense attorney.

Never in all His ministry did Jesus speak one unkind word to a sinner. When I heard a speaker say that decades ago, I was shocked. I thought you couldn't preach without condemning people. In fact, I set out to disprove him and spent hours poring over the four Gospels. What I found (or didn't find) revolutionized my ministry. I came to realize that only one sin will send a person to hell: rejecting Jesus Christ. When we shut the door to His love, we condemn ourselves. God isn't in the condemnation business, though. He's in the reclamation business.

Desert Storm

The devil not only slanders and accuses, he also tempts. His purpose is to distract, disqualify and destroy Spirit-anointed sons of God. He even attacked the pioneer Spirit-anointed Son of God, Jesus Christ. This encounter points the way to victory.

When Jesus came to earth, He faced Satan's enmity just like you and I do. In fact, the Son of God went looking for the rebel. The Spirit *led* (Mark uses an even stronger word, *drove*) Him into the desert at the start of His public ministry for a bare knuckles brawl with the evil one. There the tempter tried to persuade the God-man to deviate from His Father's will.

♦ Satan tempted Him to: 1) ***abuse His Sonship*** by using His anointing to satisfy personal desires. "You haven't eaten in 40 days. You're starving. Turn these stones into bread." It sounded so reasonable. In reality, the danger to Jesus was the sin of Balaam, prostituting God's call and gifts to personal enrichment. It's one of the great booby traps the servant of God faces.

♦ The devil then tried to entice his quarry to: 2) ***abort His Sonship*** by seeking power from an alternate source. "I'll give You the kingdom You seek if You'll just worship me." It's so easy for seasoned saints to counterfeit commitment, to imitate the genuine article, to take short cuts. Why wait for God to act? Why undergo the torture of spiritual discipline, obedience, suffering, and character formation? Why not opt instead for the Lite Gospel—everything you ever wanted in a Christian life … and less? Just shake yourself like Samson and pretend the power is still there.

♦ Finally Satan tempted Jesus to: 3) ***advertise His Sonship***, to sell Himself. "Man, Your Father surely hasn't laid out a very effective marketing strategy. If You'll give my ad agency Your account, we'll stage a public relations coup that'll have the populace eating out of Your hand. You just leap from the pinnacle of the temple while the crowds are watching, and the angels will snatch You up before You hit bottom. Then everyone will know You're the bonafide item." The tempter even quoted—

actually misquoted—the Bible to prove his point.

What a reasonable, helpful friend the fiend made himself appear. The angel of light had never seemed more radiant. Jesus wasn't buying it, however. The last Adam, unlike the first one, quashed the serpent's overtures. How? By recognizing the enemy's tactics and using heaven's weaponry. Jesus torpedoed the devil the same way we can lick him, through the power of the Spirit and the keen edge of God's sword, the Word. We must make sure that we don't sign on with the "Simon, the Sorcerer, Advertising Agency" (Acts 8: 9-13).

A Sifting and a Salvaging

Finally, the scheme Satan used on Simon Peter was sifting (Luke 22:31, 32). "Simon, Simon," Jesus predicted, "Satan has asked to sift you as wheat." "Sift" means to pour through a sieve, to scatter, or to place under intense pressure. Peter was going to be shaken and shattered. When the sifting came, he would wilt like a rose in the Sahara. Cursing like the sailor he had been, he would renounce all connection with Christ. The disciple would become a deserter and a disaster.

That's not the end of the story, however. Jesus continued, "But I have prayed for you, Simon, that your faith may not fail. And when you have turned back, strengthen your brothers." "When," not "if." When the enemy hits us with everything he can, Christ is praying for us. Rooting for us. Fighting for us. And when the devil shakes us to our toes, the Lord will restore us and return us to the front lines of kingdom combat.

What a thrilling story this is for all of us who've stumbled badly along the heavenly trail. When Beelzebub trips us up, the Lord picks us up. The final word in Peter's life isn't found in Luke or any of the Gospels, but in his courageous leadership in Acts and his marvelous epistles. *When* you have turned back, Simon. *When* ....

Satan slanders; God shoots straight.

Satan accuses; God affirms.

Satan tempts; God triumphs.

Satan sifts; God salvages.

Will you allow the schemer to play his con games and trick you out of God's promises?

No!

Price too high.

Any housewife knows that the best way to remember the things she meant to do and forgot is to start praying. They will come to her and divert her from prayer. The devil will let a preacher prepare a sermon if it will keep him from preparing himself.

—*Vance Havner*

When we do ill, the devil tempteth us; when we do nothing, we tempt him.

—*Thomas Fuller*

The preacher brings a report from the battlefield of the conflict between Christ and Satan. The news is that for the whole of mankind Jesus Christ has won the victory in His death and resurrection.

—*James W. Cox*

7

God's Armor

A cartoon by Doug Hall (*Leadership*, Winter '83) pictures a bespectacled gentleman in pinstriped suit, peering nervously through the window of a classroom door labeled "Four-Year-Olds." Under the man's left arm is a Bible. Clenched in his right hand is a box of doughnuts. The caption to the cartoon reads: "Armed to the teeth, Sunday school teacher Nat Willowby prepares to do battle with the forces of darkness."

If you've ever worked with children, you're chuckling right now. Some of you may even suspect that the prophet Daniel actually was thrown, not into a lions' den but into a classroom of hyper, hollering kids. At least that version sounds scarier to you.

The perils of teaching four-year-olds notwithstanding, spiritual warfare demands weaponry more substantial than a pack of pastries. We're not enrolled in some fantasy baseball camp for middle-aged, pot-bellied couch potatoes. This is the major leagues. This is cosmic combat. We'd better be armed with God's standard-issue military gear if we expect to conquer the real forces of darkness.

The apostle Paul tells us how to suit up properly for battle. Like a field general before a big showdown, the author of Ephesians offers final, specific instructions to his troops (6:10-20):

> Finally, be strong in the Lord and in his mighty power. Put on the full armor of God so that you can take your stand against the devil's schemes. For our struggle is not against flesh and blood, but against the rulers, against the authorities, against the powers of this dark world and against the spiritual forces of evil in the heavenly realms. Therefore put on the full armor of God, so that when the day of evil comes, you may be able to stand your ground, and after you have done everything, to stand. Stand firm then, with the belt of truth buckled around your waist, with the breastplate of righteousness in place, and with your feet fitted with the readiness that comes from the gospel of peace. In addition to all this, take up the shield of faith, with

> which you can extinguish all the flaming arrows of the evil one. Take the helmet of salvation and the sword of the Spirit, which is the word of God. And pray in the Spirit on all occasions with all kinds of prayers and requests. With this in mind, be alert and always keep on praying for all the saints.
>
> Pray also for me, that whenever I open my mouth, words may be given me so that I will fearlessly make known the mystery of the gospel, for which I am an ambassador in chains. Pray that I may declare it fearlessly, as I should.

Paul was a decorated veteran of spiritual warfare. He recognized the enemy. He possessed a profound grasp of the eternal scope of this conflict. But he also understood the spiritual resources God had given him—and all the righteous—to wage and win the war.

Well-acquainted was the apostle with the diabolical one's tactics. How he shifts back and forth between intimidation and insinuation. How he alternately plays the roles of bully and beguiler. How he employs both force and fraud. How he can appear either as a roaring lion or an angel of light. How he defies expectations and eludes grasp as effectively as Fran Tarkenton used to scramble away from opposing linemen. How hell's quarterback constantly mixes his plays, shows different looks, and uses reverses and fakes to keep the saints off-balance.

Paul also was intimately acquainted with heaven's Commander in Chief, and therefore knew the war was actually already won, the enemy defeated. Like a beleaguered Germany in the closing days of the European front of World War II, defeat for the fiend's forces was no longer in doubt. Beyond that, the Commander in Chief had provided his soldiers with all the weapons needed to prosecute safely the remaining battles and wipe out all pockets of resistance. All that was needed was for God's people to use His armaments —not their own—as instructed. And they must use the complete armor, not just certain pieces (it is not a matter of pick and choose).

"Put on the full armor of God," Paul coaches, "so that you can take your stand against the devil's schemes .... so that when the day of evil comes, you may be able to stand your ground, and after you have done everything, to stand." It's no accident that the word *stand* is repeated. To remain on one's feet is the sign of victory in the wrestling or boxing match, and the mark of survival on the battlefield. God will certainly win, but He doesn't want us to become casualties.

With what type of armor does God equip us? The apostle employs the military gear of his day as a metaphor, things like belt, breastplate, footwear, shield, helmet, and sword. Seven items come in these verses (though some commentators include only six).

The first three are fixed pieces of protection. "Stand therefore, *having* girded your loins ... *having* put on the breastplate ... *having* shod your feet" (RSV, italics added). Sandals, belt, and breastplate were worn at all times by the Roman soldier on active duty. They represent armor that belongs to us as believers.

The next three—helmet, shield, sword—were not attached to the body but were picked up when needed for fighting. They represent weaponry which is available to us at all times but must be utilized to be effective.

The final item is prayer. It stands apart from the rest and to some extent is used in connection with the other six. Prayer is like a canopy which covers all the other armature.

The Bible Belt

Paul calls the first piece *the belt of truth*. In the ancient world the belt or girdle was absolutely essential to the man-of-arms. Everyone wore long flowing robes. Before going to work, or to war, a man must gather his loose garment and bind it to his body. Failure to do so invited inconvenience and even danger. Wearing the belt streamlined one's clothing and allowed for unhindered movement.

Truth is the Christian's belt. This doesn't refer to our telling the truth, though Christians ought to be scrupulous about that. Your honesty or candor isn't what protects you against the prince of lies. Rather, its *the* truth. God's truth. The rock-solid, immutable, immovable, impenetrable reality of the Eternal One that binds and gathers and protects our spirit.

"I *am* the way and the truth and the life," Jesus asserted (John 14:6, italics added).

"The truth will set you free," He promised (John 8:36).

"Sanctify them by the truth" Christ prayed (John 17:17); your word is truth."

"Gird up the loins of your mind," Peter teaches (1 Peter 1:13).

The word is *logos*: the Word of God. The Bible is God's written revelation, and Jesus is God's incarnate revelation. He is the truth fleshed-out, come-to-life, in living Technicolor with Dolby surround sound. As John begins his gospel, "In the beginning was the Word, and the Word was with God, and the Word was God ... In him was life, and that life was the light of men .... The Word became flesh and made his dwelling among us. We have seen his glory, the glory of the One and Only, who came from the Father, full of grace and truth" (John 1:1, 4, 14).

The belt of truth holds everything in place. Christ's warriors must possess a thorough knowledge of the Word and a complete commitment to its authority. We must allow it the final word in every argument, every doctrine, every issue. By its parameters we evaluate our finances, social involvements, vocations, family life, leisure choices, ethics. Everything is bound up by this girdle.

No wonder the psalmist penned in one place, "I have hidden your word in my heart that I might not sin against you" (Psalm 119:11). And in another setting he wrote that the words of the Lord "are more precious than gold, than much pure gold; they are sweeter than honey, than honey from the comb. By them is your servant warned; in keeping them there is great reward" (Psalm 19:10, 11). No believer will triumph over Satan and his hosts without girding his/her mind up with the truth. Spiritual victory starts with the Bible belt.

One of Satan's chief tactics is to keep us from reading and studying the Bible. Biblical illiteracy plagues the contemporary Church like a spiritual polio, crippling Christian vitality. Even with all the versions and innovative packaging of God's Word that keeps it a best-seller, for many Christians it's a "seldom-read-er." The dust gathering on Bibles on shelves symbolizes the dust collecting on the spirits of Wordless disciples.

Another of the liar's ruses is to distort God's Word to the point people miss what the Lord's really telling them. For those who won't ignore the Bible, he tries to rob them of its power. The devil loves to twist and cheapen the truth. If he can turn 50,000-watt stadium lights of revelation into 5-watt night lamps, he will defuse our discipleship. Certain passages of the Bible he has turned largely into old chestnuts, robbed of their freshness and punch.

For example, many Christians apply Ephesians 2:6 to a particular worship experience, saying something like, "Didn't we sit in heavenly places today?" That's a nice sentiment. Unfortunately, it trivializes the powerful truth of that verse. Paul isn't talking about a worship "buzz" but our status as believers. We are spiritually seated already in heaven at the

Father's right hand. In Christ we've already died, risen, ascended to God's throne, and sat down beside Him. One reason we know we're going to heaven is that we're already there. Turning Mount Everest truths like that into molehill testimonies makes the evil one ecstatic.

Biblical interpretation today is rife with gimmicks and fads. Preachers love to make some verse or passage the hook to hang their whole ministry on, particularly if it brings in the people and money. Minor doctrines and misinterpreted passages become major teachings. A lot of nutty notions are making the rounds in the name of biblical truth.

"The time will come," 2 Timothy 4:3 (NEB) predicts, "when they will not stand wholesome teaching, but will follow their own fancy and gather a crowd of teachers to tickle their ears." In such an era the Church needs workmen who "correctly handle the word of truth," warriors of God who, through study of the God-breathed Scriptures, are "thoroughly equipped for every good work" (2 Timothy 4:16, 17; 2:15).

The Flak Jacket

Every Roman fighter wore a breastplate which reached approximately from his neck to his thigh and shielded his vital organs from injury. Righteousness, the old spiritual warrior explains, is our vital covering. He doesn't mean righteous living, though like telling the truth, that is a good thing. Your godliness, as fine as it may be after years of walking with God, is too full of holes to protect you from the dragon's fiery blasts.

"We couldn't carry this off by our own efforts," Paul preaches (Philippians 3:3, 4, 8, 9, Peterson), "even though we can list what many think are impressive credentials." Then he lists his degrees and pedigree, a resumé guaranteed to get him into the Pharisees' Hall of Fame. However, he continues, "I've dumped it all in the trash so that I could embrace Christ and be embraced by him. I didn't want some petty, inferior brand of righteousness that comes from keeping a list of rules when I could get the robust kind that comes from trusting Christ—*God's* righteousness."

Our breastplate isn't *imparted* righteousness but *imputed.* That's the acceptance we have, the "not guilty" verdict we've received, because of Christ's substitutionary suffering on our behalf. "God made him who had no sin to be sin for us, so that in him we might become the righteousness of God" (2 Corinthians 5:21).

Jesus made a "prince and the pauper" trade with us. He became what he was not so that we might become what we were not. As thoroughly as he became sin, just that extensively I became righteous. From top to bottom. Stem to stern. Backwards and forwards. "Who will bring any charge against those whom God has chosen?" Paul quizzes (Romans 8:33). "It is God who justifies."

If you don't understand this distinction, if you find yourself sweating over whether you've been "good enough" rather than resting on whether Christ is good enough, the accuser will make you his perpetual punching bag. Here many conscientious Christians stumble. Determined to walk a separated, sanctified path, they slip into thinking their acceptance with God depends on points they've accumulated. I have news for such folks: God doesn't operate on a point system. Even if He did, you and I could never pile up enough of them to offset the black spots on our records.

You'll never possess a protection or perfection of your own adequate for the spiritual war zone. Only Christ's righteousness meets the criteria. In the words of Augustus Toplady's *Rock of Ages*:

Nothing in my hand I bring,
Simply to Thy cross I cling;
Naked, come to Thee for dress,
Helpless, look to Thee for grace;
Foul, I to the fountain fly,
Wash me, Savior, or I die!

God's breastplate protects us from the roller-coaster rides of our emotions. It shields us from over-reliance on personal experience. It helps repel doubt and discouragement. Monitoring my feelings and evaluating my performance can really land me in quicksand, for emotions and efforts often don't measure up. Clothing myself in Christ's righteousness, however, pulls me out of the pits and plants my feet on solid rock. *The* solid Rock:

His oath, His covenant, His blood
Support me in the whelming flood;
When all around my soul gives way,
He then is all my hope and stay.
On Christ the solid Rock I stand;
All other ground is sinking sand,
All other ground is sinking sand.

All other ground. Only *His* breastplate adequately protects our vital spiritual organs from the devil's daggers.

Those Gospel Shoes

The Roman infantryman's footwear consisted of a sandal with heavy leather or wooden sole, the bottom of which contained hobnails or studs. It attached to the foot by heavy leather straps. The studs provided the soldier sure footing, and the heavy sole protected him from sharp objects, which were often planted by the enemy to pierce the feet of advancing troops. In addition, since the campaigns of Alexander the Great, mobility had been a basic strategy of war. The sandals made for lighter, quicker feet than other footwear.

Christians should always be sporting the sandals of the gospel of peace. We should be mobile fighters, flexible and quick to respond with the gospel message, yet sure-footed and durable in His service. Steady and ready. "How beautiful on the mountains," sings the prophet, "are the feet of those who bring good news, who proclaim peace, who bring good tidings, who proclaim salvation, who say to Zion, 'Your God reigns!'" (Isaiah 52:7) "I am not ashamed of the gospel," Paul insists, "because it is the power of God for the salvation of everyone who believes" (Romans 1:16).

Christianity is a traveling religion. From Abraham onward, God's people have been told to hit the road. "Whom shall I send?" the Holy One inquired of Isaiah, "And who will go for us?" (Isaiah 6:8) "Go and make disciples of all nations," Jesus ordered His crowd (Matthew 28:19), for "you will receive power when the Holy Spirit comes on you; and you will be my witnesses in Jerusalem, and in all Judea and Samaria, and to the ends of the earth" (Acts 1:8).

In *Glad Reunion* (Word Books, 1985), John Claypool reflects on Abraham's pilgrimage with Yahweh. "There was no settling down or 'nesting in' with this deity. He was forever on the move—that seems to be the essence of his reality .... The symbol of this kind of religion would be a hoisted sail, not an anchor; the goal is a 'promised land' out ahead, not a haven of rest."

Paul, the New Testament's road warrior, seems to be saying that mobility and adaptability are key elements in the Christian's arsenal. Sadly, the Church often lumbers like an armadillo rather than gliding like a gazelle. How slowly it changes and flexes. With what grinding of engines and scraping of gears does the body of Christ often respond to new opportunities and fresh directions. Often it seems to run with cast iron boots rather than winged-footed sandals. It's little wonder Jesus spoke of the faith to move mountains. Often the biggest mountain the Church has to move is itself.

If reaching the lost is our main mission, invasion of enemy-held hearts our battle plan, we must be ready to head anywhere, anytime, anyhow to spread the gospel message. Keep on your sandals, Paul is urging, so you can swiftly respond to evangelism openings and sure-footedly stride through Satan's turf. In our super-secularized cultures, we need creative and radical approaches to reach the lost. Many of us are better at evading the unsaved community than invading it. We stand around barefooted, behind closed sanctuary doors, wondering why sinners aren't being converted. Our lack of gospel sandals is a gospel scandal.

We need more evangelization innovations such as "night churches," congregations that worship where and when the pagan world is partying full-steam. In John Passuelo's church in Buenos Aires, Argentina, a young man came to Jesus out of the rock-and-drug culture. A few weeks later the young believer told his pastor, "I believe God wants me to go down and witness at the discothèque." Passuelo couldn't help worrying about the man's desire to return to the moral pigpen he'd just left. However, not wanting to rain on the fellow's spiritual fervor, the pastor gave his blessing.

"Of course," continued the young man, "if I'm there witnessing Saturday between midnight and 4 a.m., I won't be able to attend your 5 o'clock Sunday prayer meeting." That made Passuelo worry more.

About six weeks later the young Christian came to his pastor with another request. "I want you to preach at the discothèque.

I have permission from the owner. Most of the people there have never heard a gospel message."

"Sure, I'll do that," Passuelo replied, not as sure as he sounded.

"That's great. The time for the service is 4 o'clock in the morning. You can start preaching as soon as they close for the night."

More uncomfortable than he'd ever been, the obliging pastor showed up at the discothèque with Bible in hand (he didn't bring doughnuts). He'd never been in such a place, and the blaring music and flashing lights unnerved him further. Promptly at 4 a.m., however, the music stopped and the nightclub grew quiet. The owner climbed up on the bar and yelled, "All right, everybody, give me your attention. Preacher Passuelo is here, and he's going to talk to us about God."

Reluctant and skeptical, the pastor presented a short message while the young man who'd invited him prayed in the corner of the room. To Passuelo's shock, 35 people accepted his invitation to receive Jesus Christ, all because of the quick-hearted mobility of a wet-behind-the-ears convert who didn't know any better than to follow in Jesus' sandal prints.

How easily we forget that our Master constantly did outrageous acts like that to build bridges to the lost. And the religious establishment threw a fit over it then, like it will today if you go where the sinners are. At least you're in good company with Jesus.

An Unshakable Shield

The shield of faith is the first piece we're told to "take up." The Roman shield was large, about 2-1/2' by 4', and designed to protect the whole body. Made of wood, it was overlaid with both metal and leather linings. The soldier wielded it with his left arm. Often he would soak the leather covering in water before battle, to help fend off the flaming darts fired by enemy archers. A Roman fighter once supposedly pulled 250 of those projectiles from his shield following a clash.

Faith is the believer's shield of defense. With it we can ward off the evil one's blistering attacks. Remember God's response to Abram (later his name was change to Abraham) after he had refused to accept even a shoelace from the King of Sodom following a dramatic raid on Sodom's enemies? "Do not be afraid, Abram. I am your shield, your very great reward" (Genesis 15:1).

No wonder Abraham carries the title, "father of the faithful." He lived by faith, trusting God to provide all his needs, from an inheritance to an heir. How many, many times did he have to deflect no-account Belial's white-hot arrows of doubt and temptation. "Where's that son God promised, Abe, my man? You're sure looking old. Don't tell me you're still clinging to that pipe dream. Descendants as numerous as the stars of the heaven? Only an old fool would swallow that."

Yet Abraham swallowed. He believed even though God's promises seemed impossible. He believed even though he had no idea how or when they would be fulfilled. He believed against all evidence because he considered Him faithful who had promised (Hebrews 11:11). His shield must have stopped thousands of the deceiver's darts.

If you're convinced of God's promises, you can stop them also. And nothing can stop you. Circumstances can't. People can't. Disappointment can't. It doesn't matter how much the devil turns up the heat, your shield remains unsinged when you know the one who made the promises is absolutely reliable. Shadrach, Meshach, and Abednego (Daniel 3) can tell you the Lord offers the best fireproofing in the business. Even before they knew the outcome of their furnace tour, they stood unshaken. "God can rescue us," they told the king, "but even if we're barbecued, you can't scorch our trust in Him."

Sometimes, as God did with Abraham and Sarah, or Joseph and Mary, or Gideon, or the widow at Zarephath, He asks us to do or believe things that seem ludicrous. And they would be if "the Father of all lights, with whom there is never the slightest variation or shadow of inconsistency" (James 1:17, *Phillips*), weren't the one doing the asking.

The epic epistler must have had the shield in mind when he scrawled the sentences of Romans 8:35-39:

> Who shall separate us from the love of Christ? Shall trouble or hardship or persecution or famine or nakedness or danger or sword? As it is written: "For your sake we face death all day long; we are considered as sheep to be slaughtered." No, in all these things we are more than conquerors through him who loved us. For I am convinced that neither death nor life, neither angels nor demons, neither the present nor the future, nor any powers, neither height nor depth, nor anything else in all creation, will be able to separate us from the love of God that is in Christ Jesus our Lord.

That's *some* shield.

Heavenbound Headgear

The Roman helmet was constructed of leather and topped by a crest or plume. For protection and further ornamentation, plates or bosses of metal were added. The soldier wore his helmet only when heading off to battle or some special type of duty.

The helmet is our salvation. "Since we belong to the day, let us be self-controlled, putting on faith and love as a breastplate, and the hope of salvation as a helmet" (1 Thessalonians

5:8). "Hope" is faith looking to the future, claiming the promises of tomorrow. It is a vital catalyst in our salvation, allowing us to persevere to the end of our spiritual journey. "For God did not appoint us to suffer wrath," the passage continues, "but to receive salvation through our Lord Jesus Christ. He died for us so that, whether we are awake or asleep, we may live together with him. Therefore encourage one another and build each other up, just as in fact you are doing" (5:9-11).

How about a little grammar lesson? Salvation includes three tenses. 1) Believers *have been saved.* It's a done deal. Jesus has paid the penalty for sins, and we are declared "not guilty" by faith and delivered from Satan. That's *justification.*

2) Christians *are being saved.* "Continue to work out your salvation with fear and trembling," God's Word directs (Philippians 2:12, 13), "for it is God who works in you to will and to act according to his good purpose." We are "human becomings"—growing in grace and the knowledge of the Lord Jesus Christ. That's *sanctification.*

3) God's people *will be saved.* "Now we are children of God," John encourages (1 John 3:2), "and what we will be has not yet been made known. But we know that when he appears, we shall be like him, for we shall see him as he is." That's *glorification.*

"For God has not destined us to the terrors of judgment, but to the *full attainment* of salvation through our Lord Jesus Christ" (1 Thessalonians 5:9, NEB, italics added). Believers have their eyes glued on eternity. The salvation we taste now is just the appetizer. The best is yet to be. The "hope of glory" surrounds our mind like a helmet, anchoring it amid the doubts, questions, and worries of this present world.

A Spirit-Sharpened Sword

Two Greek terms are translated "word" in the New

Testament. One is *logos*, the eternal, unchanging, comprehensive truth of God. That objective revelation is the girdle that binds up the mind and spirit. The other one, used in verse 17, is *rhema*. In a sense the two words are the same. Yet, generally speaking, *rhema* refers to the spoken Word of God, given at a certain time for a specific purpose. The *rhema* is a byte of the *logos*, e-mailed to your heart just when you need it. It's the pinpoint thrust of the Spirit's sword at a particular moment. You've experienced that, haven't you?

So have I. When my dad died, I stood at night alone in the room with his corpse. In my solitary grief I reached over and placed my hands on his head. It felt cold and hard as a rock. Suddenly the reality that he was gone overwhelmed me. In that moment of wrenching grief, the passage from 2 Corinthians 5 flashed like lightning through my mind: "If our earthly house of this tabernacle be dissolved, we have a building of God, a house not made with hands, eternal in the heavens." I threw up my hands and began praising God. Then I went back home and underlined that passage—I suppose I've marked it in every Bible I've owned. God gave me just the *rhema* I needed at that moment of heartbreak.

Please remember two things that will prevent abuses and excesses of this principle. First, the *rhema* always comes from the *logos*. The subjective proceeds from the objective. I don't "name it and claim it;" God names it and I claim it. Any "word from the Lord" must measure up to the Word of the Lord.

Second, *rhema* always comes from the Spirit of God. He's the delivery vehicle. The Word and the Spirit always work in tandem. Word without spirit produces death. Spirit without word produces disaster. Together they produce deliverance.

"The sword of the Spirit" is a *rhema* word from God, God's razor-sharp saber wielded by the Holy Spirit's hand with surgical accuracy. It pierces the enemy through, rescuing the Christian combatant in the heat of battle. The classic example is Jesus' desert duel with the devil (Matthew 4:1-11).

When Satan tempted the weak and vulnerable God-man, Jesus rebutted His adversary with words from the Word, handed Him from Deuteronomy by the very Spirit who had driven Him there. "If you are the Son of God," cackled the tempter, "tell these stones to become bread."

"It is written," countered the Master: "'Man does not live on bread alone, but on every word that comes from the mouth of God.'"

"If you are the Son of God, throw yourself down."

"It is also written: 'Do not put the Lord your God to the test.'"

"All this I will give you, if you will bow down and worship me."

"It is written: 'Worship the Lord your God, and serve Him only.'"

"It is written … It is written …."—devastating strikes of the Spirit's sword. Just what Jesus needed at those moments. That's why it's critical for us to wear the belt of truth, to have the Word of God, "living and active, sharper than any two-edged sword" (Hebrews 4:12), thoroughly stashed away inside. When the enemy attacks, the Spirit can quickly put the cutlass in our grasp and guide its thrusts.

Know the Word. Keep your sword close at hand.

The Weapon of Prayer

Without this tool our armor is incomplete. "And pray in the Spirit on all occasions with all kinds of prayers and requests … be alert and always keep on praying for all the saints. Pray also for me … that I will fearlessly make known the mystery of the gospel" (vv. 18, 19). Pray all the time. Pray in all situations. Pray all kinds of prayers. Pray!

Prayer is the soldier's communication system with Supreme Command. It keeps us in touch with "headquarters." It allows us to receive fresh orders and instructions. It keeps us informed of the enemy's activities.

"Pray in the Spirit" means supernatural, God-fueled intercession. Like the hot air balloon lifts its passengers into the sky, the Spirit fires our petitions and boosts them heavenward. Don't miss the "oomph" of Romans 8:26, 27. "In the same way, the Spirit helps us in our weakness. We do not know what we ought to pray for, but the Spirit himself intercedes for us with groans that words cannot express. And he who searches our hearts knows the mind of the Spirit, because the Spirit intercedes for the saints in accordance with God's will."

And people think the *Internet* is amazing? It's stone age compared to prayer in the Spirit.

Perhaps this is one of the chief reasons for the gift of tongues. When God can bypass our puny little brains, prejudices and other "filters" to run a direct line from our hearts to His heart, tremendous things can happen. "When we cannot choose words in order to pray properly, the Spirit Himself expresses our pleas in a way that could never be put into words" (Romans 8:26, *Phillips*).

We have a prayer partner who travels with us everywhere we go. Anytime we don't know how to express ourselves to God properly, He can pray for us. Isn't that wonderful? Sometimes we pray and pray until victory comes, and we know we've connected with heaven's throne in a prevailing way, yet rationally we don't even comprehend exactly what it is we've been praying about. However, we know that our heart has meshed with the heart of our Father. "I don't know what to say" has become "Hallowed be thy name, thy kingdom come, thy will be done." An important battle has been won.

Once I was praying for another person. He had been

obstinate and difficult to deal with. He stood directly in the way of what I felt God was trying to do. I prayed for him (or *at* him) until I ran out of words and gas. My petitions seemed to be bouncing back in my face.

Then the Spirit took over, quickly taking my prayers from zero to 60 mph. A powerful sense of release began to fill my spirit. Then I "heard" the Lord's voice. "Do you know what you've just been praying? You're the one that needs changing, not he. Once you allowed the Spirit to take the wheel, your prayers could start working on the fellow who really needs it."

That's a weapon, folks. You can conquer the enemy with that, even when the enemy is you. As Dwight L. Moody quipped, "I have never met a man who has given me as much trouble as myself." But whoever the opposition, potent prayer along with the rest of God's armor can enable you to "stand your ground, and after you have done everything, to stand."

A New Year's Day. The breathtaking Tournament of Roses parade. Right in the middle of the route, a large float sputtered to a stop. The entire parade was stopped until someone could fetch a can of gas. The sponsor of the float? Standard Oil Company. The spectators laughed at the irony of a huge oil company's float running out of gas.

The King of the universe has put all His resources at our disposal. We have no excuse for running on empty or being caught with our guard down. Let's arm ourselves to the teeth and prepare to do battle with the forces of darkness.

Wherever God erects a house of prayer,
The Devil always builds a chapel there;
And 'twill be found, upon examination,
The latter has the largest congregation.

—Daniel Defoe

Learning without piety will only make you more capable of promoting the kingdom of Satan.

—George Whitefield

Religion is the best armor a man can have, but it is the worst cloak.

—John Bunyan

8

Demolishing Strongholds

Thousands of castles dot the landscape of modern Europe. Built during the Middle Ages, they protected local feudal nobles and their families. Their towering and massive (sometimes 30 feet thick) walls, often perched on mountainsides and surrounded by moats, made them almost impregnable. Their imposing presence centuries later testifies to their formidability.

These medieval fortresses also helped lords dominate the

lands around them. A well-placed castle could control critical river crossings, mountain passes, or sea harbors. When a monarch wanted to expand his power to new areas, he constructed fortresses there also. Peasants living nearby became his vassals.

Have you realized that Satan operates toward the Church like a feudal lord? He attempts to fill the terrain with his castles and dominate everything and everyone within his reach. Many, many Christians, because they do not understand spiritual things, live under the bondage of strongholds—oftentimes very religious strongholds—built by the evil one. Convinced they have nothing to do with the devil, these folks unwittingly live under his influence. They think his thoughts and do his deeds like loyal vassals, unaware that they're dwelling in the shadow of Lord Belial's castle.

The prince of sinners has more religion than many church members have. His strongholds are whatever will keep people from knowing Jesus Christ and living in His victory. If religion will do that—and it often does—Satan happily employs it. Therefore demonic spirits probably operate in church more than any other place. They don't need to give unbelievers that much attention, for they're already in the devil's hip pocket. Among Christians, however, those spirits work feverishly, trying to gain a foothold in Christ's camp.

Please don't hear what's not being said; Christians cannot be demon-possessed. Evil spirits cannot own Christians because they are God's property. He already resides there and He doesn't sublease. But don't assume that, because you're God's child, you don't have to deal with demonic powers. Satan's emissaries can impact your life and ministry in other ways. Remember how well-organized the dragon's kingdom is? His minions operate with extreme efficiency in penetrating the righteous ranks and constructing citadels of evil influence which oppose the mind and will of God.

Levels of Lucifer's Operation

Consider these six levels of demonic activity identified by D. G. Kehl (*Demon Possession*, edited by John Warwick Montgomery, Bethany House Publishers, Minneapolis, Minnesota, 1976, pp. 121, 122):

1) ***Demonic impression***—thoughts, ideas, and perceptions that distract one's mind from the truth. Often they seem to come "out of nowhere," filtering in like stray radio signals to disturb our reception of God's Spirit.

2) ***Demonic repression***—suppression of one's response to the truth. Jesus compared it to seed that falls on hardened ground and never gets the chance to put down roots (Matthew 13:19). "When anyone hears the message about the kingdom and does not understand it, the evil one comes and snatches away what was sown in his heart." The Word of God does not remain in the heart long enough to accomplish any good. Or, it may be the repression of a memory that gives the enemy a stronghold in one's life.

3) ***Demonic obsession***—preoccupation with demonic impressions. Like a heat-seeking missile, a person gets locked in on a suspicion, fear, hurt, attraction, or other unhealthy thought pattern. The impressions are not dismissed but embraced. They lodge in the mind and spirit and grow like cancer. I know of a pastor whose failure in ministry was due almost entirely to his obsession that others were out to get him.

Frederick Buechner describes the results of one such preoccupation (*Wishful Thinking*, Harper & Row, 1973). "Of the Seven Deadly Sins, anger is possibly the most fun. To lick your wounds, to smack your lips over grievances long past, to roll over your tongue the prospect of bitter confrontations still to come, to savor to the last toothsome morsel both the pain you are given and the pain you are giving back—in many ways it is a feast fit for a king. The chief drawback is that what you are wolfing down is yourself. The skeleton at the feast is you."

4) ***Demonic depression***—strangling discouragement that comes not from medical or circumstantial sources, but which can only be ascribed to spiritual assault. Or it can hitchhike onto other types of depression, multiplying the pain. Call it *devilpression.* It's deep, it's dark, it's devastating. The suffering intensifies with the guilt felt: *if I were the Christian I should be, I wouldn't feel this way.* Interestingly, church history informs us that many great women and men of faith over the centuries battled depression.

5) ***Demonic oppression***—an all-out blitzkrieg by the enemy. Hell's forces storm from every angle, throwing wave after wave of attack in an attempt to paralyze you.

6) ***Demonic possession***—an evil spirit (or spirits) takes up residence within the human spirit, leaving an individual totally under Satan's control. Despite the attention this receives in some areas of church and society today, probably few people experience this level. The devil may even avoid this option much of the time because it's so obvious, and he prefers to traffic in subtlety and deception.

Mind Games

Where does the wicked one build his bastions of influence, his walled towers of opposition to God's workings? In the mind. The human brain is one of the Creator's most marvelous gifts to humanity. With its amazing abilities to understand, to reason, to imagine, to create, it sets us above all else in God's creation. Therefore the prince of darkness and his subordinates want most to establish their strongholds in the minds of individuals, in the mindsets of cultures, and in the thought patterns of the Church. Spiritual warfare is a battle for the mind.

As 2 Corinthians 10:3-5 words it: "For though we live in the world, we do not wage war as the world does. The weapons we fight with are not the weapons of the world. On the contrary, they have divine power to demolish strongholds. We demolish arguments and every pretension that sets itself up against the knowledge of God, and we take captive every thought to make it obedient to Christ."

According to the apostle Paul, God furnishes believers with spiritual weapons to pull down the fortresses or strongholds of the devil. The Mighty One gives us power, in the words of various translations, to bulldoze false *imaginations*, *speculations*, *mindsets*, *reasonings*, *thoughts*, *deceptions*, *arrogance*, and *arguments*. All these descriptive terms refer to mental processes. As John Milton penned, "The mind is its own place, and in itself can make a Heav'n of Hell, a Hell of Heav'n." That's where we win or lose the spiritual battle. That's where the archfiend attempts to establish his fortifications.

It's no wonder, then, that Jesus repeatedly stressed the command of Deuteronomy 6:5. "Love the Lord your God with all your heart and with all your soul and with all your *mind*. This is the first and greatest commandment" (Matthew 22:37, 38, italics added).

When God saves someone, Jesus was emphasizing, He saves the whole person. He wants His castle to control the whole being, the body and the mind and the spirit. He wants the entire person to be transformed and to conform to His loving grace. Contrarily, Satan loves to create unbalanced Christians who are stunted in one or more of those areas. Nothing distorts the reality of saving truth more than a poorly-proportioned saint.

Some people's religion is all mental. They think Christianity is merely a matter of learning doctrine inside and out. The scribes were like that, as were the disciples of scholasticism centuries later. That's *intellectualism*.

Others become preoccupied with the emotions, living by

feelings and gauging theirs and others' spirituality by the mood of the moment. They worship and live for the next spiritual high. Now emotion is a vital link in spirituality, an often neglected one—why can't we get as excited about Jesus as we do over our favorite football team or entertainer? When feelings become the locomotive that pulls the train, however, the result is *emotionalism.*

Still others make the faith a matter of willpower: whoever punishes self the most or follows the strictest rules is the best Christian. The Pharisees of Christ's day had developed a system of ritual and regulation as dense and intimidating as an African jungle. That's *legalism.*

God, though, wants a whole person. A well-proportioned disciple. As pastor and professor John Swails once observed, "Develop the physical alone, and you have an animal. Develop the intellect alone and you have a self-serving atheistic isolationist. Develop the spiritual alone and you have a religious fanatic. Develop the physical, the intellectual, and the spiritual components equally, and you have a person who is strong to the work, intelligent in his direction, and dedicated to God and his calling."

The Lord urgently wants our minds, as well as our spirits and bodies, in top-notch shape to serve Him. How we think controls how we talk and act. If we don't think right, we won't be right or live right. The Gettysburg of spiritual warfare is fought in our minds.

Three Enemies

In Colossians 2, Paul warns of three strongholds. Hear his cautionary comments:

1) Don't let anyone "take you captive through hollow and deceptive philosophy" (2:8).

2) Don't "let anyone judge you" by what rules or traditions

you keep or fail to keep (2:16).

3) Don't let anyone "disqualify you for the prize" (2:18). These are three strongholds Lucifer builds in the Church—control, condemnation, and cowardice.

♦ ***Control*** (*Don't let anyone take you captive*). The Bible says we were saved to freedom. "If the Son sets you free, you will be free indeed" (John 8:36). "Through Christ Jesus the law of the Spirit of life set me free from the law of sin and death" (Romans 8:2). Christ's atonement is our emancipation proclamation. We're not under bondage to anybody.

Don't let people imprison you with their counterfeit philosophies or human traditions, for such persons are motivated by "the elemental spirits of the universe" (2:8), a better translation than "basic principles." According to Paul, these evil forces control the false doctrine he's referring to here.

These demons use religion, "the traditions of men," to dominate the Church. This stronghold of control often chokes the life out of a congregation. In some churches one or two people control everything that happens: in worship, in ministry, in the organization. Always that will deteriorate into something destructive and hurtful. Satan uses the strangleholds of excessive and unhealthy traditions and domineering personalities to shackle the saints and stifle the flow of the Spirit. They become a walled castle making vassals out of redeemed people.

♦ ***Condemnation*** (*Don't let anyone judge you*). There's always someone ready to pass sentence on your behavior, to condemn you for failing to observe their nit-picking rules ("Don't handle this! Don't taste that! Don't touch those!"). They'll nail you for the way you dress, for the style of your worship, for the places you go. They'll blast you for the car you drive, for the people you befriend, even for the version of the Bible you use. Judgmentalism constructs thicker walls than just about anything, and it stocks its moats with man-eating crocodiles. Why, legalists will even build blockades in front of heaven's door and keep folks from going in (Matthew 23:13, 14).

Here's a secret that can liberate you from that fortress. When people judge you, let it remain their problem, not yours. We're called to be salt, but God doesn't expect us to be pretzels, twisting ourselves in knots to satisfy everyone's expectations of us.

I was ministering at a conference in North Carolina years ago when a man with more hang-ups than a barrel of fish-hooks confronted me. "Your hair's too long," he blustered. "When are you going to cut it?"

"When I get ready," I retorted.

"I love your preaching," he continued, "but I hate your looks."

I answered, "Then *you've* got the problem, brother, not I."

Don't let anyone judge you—those are God's words, not man's, the same God who announces that "there is now no condemnation for those who are in Christ Jesus" (Romans 8:1). The same Lord who looked into the face of an adulterous woman and announced, "I don't condemn you, either."

♦ ***Cowardice*** (*Don't let anyone disqualify you*). The specific danger Paul addresses here is the super-spiritualist, the person who wears his visions and other sensational experiences like a general wears war medals. Who attempts to lord it over the less mystical (and thus inferior) saints.

Don't misunderstand; visions and dreams can be genuine. But they are never meant to disqualify others who may not move as easily in the mystical realm. Neither should they be used to lord it over others. True words from the Lord will harmonize with Scripture, and they will build up the Body. When personal experience is used to exalt self and disparage others' spirituality, it becomes the devil's tool. We need to guard against denigrating those whose worship or experience doesn't seem as high-octane as our own.

God has not given us a spirit of fear (2 Timothy 1:7). We shouldn't succumb to a loser's mentality because someone else rules us out of the race. Whoever does that is the one out of line, the unspiritual one. "He has lost connection with the Head, from whom the whole body, supported and held together by its ligaments and sinews, grows as God causes it to grow" (Colossians 2:19). Overdoses of mysticism, emotionalism, and super-spirituality can oppress the work of God as severely as a cold, controlling environment can.

A Loser's Mentality

Many churches and people are not moving with God because Satan's strongholds dominate the landscape, ruling every passageway through which the Spirit would move. There are spirits of control—slave spirits. They operate through persons who are determined to rule or ruin. There are spirits of condemnation—judgmental spirits. They work through guilt mongers who censure others' lifestyle and behavior. There are spirits of conceit—paralyzing spirits. They operate through supercilious souls who look down their noses at everyone else's walk with God.

Because of Satan's strategic stockades, churches can fall far beneath their God-ordained potential. They fizzle in worship. They're feeble with discipleship. They fail at community. They flounder in outreach. God's not glorified, believers aren't sanctified, the Church isn't edified, and the lost aren't evangelized. If those congregations don't weed out those critical and condemning spirits, and wipe out the spirits of shame and false guilt, and tear down those spirits of fear and intimidation, they'll miss the victories Christ has already won for them.

And because of these strongholds, individual Christians needlessly live defeated existences. They are bound up, guilt-ridden, self-loathing. They've been hoodwinked by the enemy until they're neutralized, hypnotized, and paralyzed. They're brainwashed believers, of little use on the battlefield of spiritual warfare. Even when the clouds of despair momentarily lift, these people just know it won't last. They have become experts at snatching defeat from the jaws of victory.

In the sports world, it's known as a loser's mentality. Coaches and scouts and general managers have found that attitude has as much to do with winning as ability. What sets apart the Magic Johnsons and Michael Jordans and Joe Montanas? Their insatiable desire to win and belief they will win. Therefore in player trades and drafts, teams have learned to dump the "loser" and snag the "winner," the athlete who will infect the whole program with his positive passion. Sports history is replete with stories of "ordinary" squads that performed extraordinarily because of their winner's mindset.

In the same way, some pastors find success and build great churches not because they're more gifted or dedicated than their peers but because they own that winner's heart. We look at them and think, "I can preach as good as he can. I've got more training than he does. How does he do it?" It's the mindset.

God wants all His children to be winners. "We are more than conquerors through him who loved us" (Romans 8:37). "I can do everything through Christ who gives me strength" (Philippians 4:13). "Thanks be to God, who always leads us in triumphal procession in Christ and through us spreads everywhere the fragrance of the knowledge of him" (2 Corinthians 2:14).

Reflecting on horrendous personal trials, Paul writes, "We are hard-pressed on all sides, but we are never frustrated; we are puzzled, but never in despair. We are persecuted, but are never deserted; we may be knocked down but we are never knocked out!" (2 Corinthians 4:8, 9, *Phillips*). Even if Satan takes the first quarter, God's squad will rebound in the second. And you can mark it down: the King of kings *owns* the fourth quarter. The final score will reflect a blowout.

Storm the Fort

What do we do with these fortresses of demonic thinking that choke and chill and cheat the followers of the Lord Jesus? Pull them down with the weapons of our warfare. Employ heaven's wrecking crew. Go after Beelzebub's bulwarks with bulldozer and battering ram. Attack his strongholds like Rome sacked Carthage, leveling them and then salting the soil of our minds with God's victorious truth so the devil's deception won't grow there again.

Listen to Paul's preaching once more (2 Corinthians 10:3-6, Peterson):

> The world is unprincipled. It's dog-eat-dog out there. The world doesn't fight fair. But we don't live or fight our battles that way—never have and never will. The tools of our trade aren't for marketing or manipulation, but they are for demolishing that entire massively corrupt culture. We use our powerful God-tools for smashing warped philosophies, tearing down barriers erected against the truth of God, fitting every loose thought and emotion and impulse into the structure of life shaped by Christ. Our tools are ready at hand for clearing the ground of every obstruction and building lives of obedience into maturity.

How do we pull down the enemy's bastions? Not with human weapons—arguments, legislation, programs, etc.—but with mighty, supernatural, God-given armaments. Like Jesus in the wilderness, we depend on the power of the Spirit and the truth of God's Word. Like the early apostles, we fight and live and minister in the name (authority) of Jesus Christ. Like Paul, we win the showdown for supremacy of the mind by relying on the mind of Christ.

Satan's strongholds always result in people thinking like him: needing to control, desiring to dominate, striving to exalt self and put others down. On the contrary, we are to think like Jesus thought. "Let your attitude to life be that of Christ Jesus himself," Paul urges. "For he, who had always been God by nature, did not cling to his privileges as God's equal, but stripped himself of every advantage …." (Philippians 2:5-8, *Phillips*). Contrast Jesus' mentality described in these verses with Lucifer's pictured in Isaiah 14:12-15.

The mind of the devil	**The mind of Christ**
♦ I will ascend to heaven	♦ He did not cling to His privileges as God's equal, but stripped Himself
♦ I will raise my throne above the stars of God	♦ He consented to be a slave by nature
♦ I will sit enthroned ... on the utmost heights of the sacred mountain	♦ He was born a man
♦ I will ascend above the tops of the clouds	♦ He humbled Himself by living a life of utter obedience
♦ I will make myself like the Most High	♦ He died the death of a common criminal

Jesus said that the greatest would be servant of all. He said the last would be first, and the first last. He said whoever exalted himself would be humbled, and the humble would be exalted. He said you save your life by losing it. He said you become rich by being poor. And He walked everything He talked.

Talk about a winner's mentality, divine-style. The mindset Christ modeled, ludicrous to a lost world, is in reality the only sanity. The lifestyle He practiced, repugnant to pagans, is the only path to true life. His upside-down kingdom is the only thing that's really right-side up. It's this fallen race, blinded by the dung god who tried to become first and ended up the biggest loser of all, who's really crazy and dying and turned on its head.

Colossians 2:13-15 details the Lord's total triumph over Satan's fortresses through that humiliating death on the cross. Christ has canceled the certificate of death against us (or as Hebrews 2:14, 15 puts it, "so that by his death he might destroy him who holds the power of death—that is, the devil —and free those who all their lives were held in slavery by their fear of death"). Our Savior has disarmed the devil and his hosts and declared the bankruptcy of the evil kingdom. He has made a public spectacle of His defeated foes, a victory parade through the streets of the capital, so to speak. As Ephesians 4:8 (KJV) exults, "he led captivity captive."

Don't let the despoiled demons of darkness build their scaffolding in your brain, or in the mind of your church. In the name of Jesus, by the evidence of God's Word, through the power of the Spirit, pull them down. We don't need to control things now, for the King of kings and Lord of lords is in the driver's seat. We don't need to judge one another, for the Judge of all the earth has paid the price for all our sins and accepts us in Him. We don't need to play superiority games, for the Heavenly One has neutralized all one-upmanship by His all-the-way-downmanship.

Above all, we don't need to remain blinded by the evil

one's ruses, for the "God who said, 'Let light shine out of darkness,' made His light shine in our hearts to give us the light of the knowledge of the glory of God in the face of Christ" (2 Corinthians 4:6). Using God's weapons, we can smash those "warped philosophies" and batter down the "barriers erected against the truth of God," and capture "every loose thought and emotion and impulse" for Jesus. Like Joshua and the Israelites at Jericho, we can obediently surround the enemy walls that block our path to God's promised possession and watch them come crashing to the ground. We can shout, for "the Lord has given you the city!" (Joshua 6:16).

If you travel to Europe, you can visit many of the castles that once defended lords and ladies, their families and subjects. You can marvel at the mountainous walls, the broad ramparts, the hidden passageways, the rows of swords and spears and shields. These centuries-old strongholds make fascinating tourist attractions.

That's all they are, however. Curiosities. Historical relics. They lost their effectiveness half a millennium ago with the spread of gunpowder and cannons. No sane person would consider them adequate protection against a modern army. Against tanks and missiles and jets and bombs, these fortresses are castles of sand.

Likewise, no Christian has to live in bondage to the strongholds of Satan. The weapons provided us through Christ are so much more powerful than anything the enemy has constructed. He's a defeated foe, a humiliated spectacle, a relic of those dark ages before the Light invaded. It's time God's followers kick sand in the bully's face and demolish his castles.

Who wants to join heaven's demolition crew?

Satan deals with confusion and lies. Put the truth in front of him and he is gone.

—*Paul Matlock*

Whoever recognizes the depth of his own frailty is greater than the one who sees visions of angels.

—*Isaac of Nineveh*

The line between the Spirit and the flesh is very fine and easily crossed.

—*M. D. Kelly*

9

Discerning the Spirits

It boggles the mind.

Every day billions of products roll along the assembly lines of the world's manufacturing facilities. Candy bars and cameras. Textiles and tennis balls. Automobiles and air-fresheners. They're all headed for you and me, the consumers, shipped with the confidence that we will consume. And we do, trusting that those candy bars won't poison us and the tennis balls will bounce with just the right amount of spring.

What gives the producers their confidence and us consumers our trust? Two words: *quality control.* They describe a critical component of manufacturing. Somewhere in the process from design to delivery, someone is examining the finished product to verify that it passes inspection. Someone carries the assignment of insuring that only first-quality merchandise leaves the factory with the company name and reputation riding on it.

Of course many people are addicted bargain hunters. Maybe you're one of them. You comb outlet stores and discount marts looking for items that didn't quite pass quality control but still are worth buying (especially at a much lower price). Many of those "seconds" seem perfect—only an expert could find the flaw. Nevertheless, it exists, and the retailer doesn't try to pull the wool over your eyes (or your neck). That's why you're able to buy a $50 sweater for $12.95.

Other businessmen are wool-pullers. They make a bundle selling shoddy imitations of everything from cassettes to cookware to cologne. To the novice shopper, these fakes look or sound or feel like the genuine articles, when in fact they're cheap rip-offs. Let the buyer beware.

The Church desperately needs a system of spiritual quality control. The Spirit is manufacturing "marvelous" things in our day, but Satan, the master bamboozler, continues to pander his pirated versions. In addition, well-intentioned but fallible believers say and do things in God's name that are spiritual "seconds."

Heaven's Quality Control

Fortunately, God has provided the Church with superb quality control procedures. Consider the following Scriptures:

"Now to each one the manifestation of the Spirit is given for the common good. To one there is given through the

Spirit the message of wisdom ... to another distinguishing between spirits ..." (1 Corinthians 12:7-10). Or as the King James version calls it, "discerning of spirits."

"Two or three prophets should speak, and the others should weigh carefully what is said" (1 Corinthians 14:29), or "pass judgment" (NASB).

"Do not put out the Spirit's fire; do not treat prophecies with contempt. Test everything. Hold on to the good. Avoid every kind of evil" (1 Thessalonians 5:19-22).

"... That you may not be quickly shaken from your composure or be disturbed either by a spirit [spiritual manifestation] or a message or a letter as if from us, to the effect that the day of the Lord has come" (2 Thessalonians 2:2).

"Dear friends, do not believe every spirit, but test the spirits to see whether they are from God, because many false prophets have gone out into the world. This is how you can recognize the Spirit of God: Every spirit that acknowledges that Jesus Christ has come in the flesh is from God, but every spirit that does not acknowledge Jesus is not from God. This is the spirit of the antichrist .... We are from God, and whoever knows God listens to us; but whoever is not from God does not listen to us. This is how we recognize the Spirit of truth and the spirit of falsehood" (1 John 4:1-3, 6).

Distinguishing between spirits, weighing carefully what is said, testing everything—this is heaven's quality control.

Let's return to the military metaphor. Spiritual combat by its very nature takes place in the spiritual realm. Understandably then, the combatants include a vast array of invisible spiritual beings. They are unseen, unrecognized, even ignored by people who lack the eye, the ear, the spirit to discern them. The Holy Spirit through the Word teaches that the evil angels under Lucifer's command are at war with the angels of God, and that this battle front forms a critical context of our campaign against evil.

Of necessity, therefore, Christians must have some method of identifying who is friend and who is enemy. To address this need God gives believers the ability to distinguish between true and false spirits, between those who serve in the King's army and those who have enlisted in the rebel forces. The gift of discernment is one of the supernatural manifestations placed in the Church's arsenal to assist it in this cosmic conflict.

A New Field General

As Commander Jesus met with a group of loyal subordinates disheartened over His imminent departure, He buoyed them with this news. "It is for your good that I am going away. Unless I go away, the Counselor will not come to you; but if I go, I will send him to you" (John 16:7). That promise, fulfilled weeks later by the risen, ascended Christ on the Day of Pentecost, keys the Church's success. The constant presence with every single soldier of another field general just like Jesus, ensures our victory. Each of us has Christ Himself, through the Spirit, accompanying us onto the field of conflict.

And this everywhere-at-once Spirit brings with Him a dazzling array of weaponry: spiritual gifts, ministry empowerments, enabling tools. You don't get just the Holy Spirit—actually we don't get Him; He gets us—but all His powers and possessions as well. That's why the Bible assures that "the one who is in you is greater than the one who is in the world" (1 John 4:4). Within each of us resides a *supernatural* Helper.

Of course, unlike Satan who gladly enslaves people, the Holy Spirit only works in cooperation with us. Our resistance can quell His effectiveness. Perhaps that's one reason good habits seem so much easier to break than bad ones. God's Spirit doesn't force prayer or Bible reading or other healthy disciplines upon us. The devil, contrariwise, delights in shackling us with destructive addictions. Bondage is his specialty.

Therefore, the Christian warrior must learn to work with the Spirit, recognize His strategies, and move in synchrony. Jesus said this Helper "will be in you," "will teach you all things, and will remind you of everything I have said to you" (John 14:17, 26). "He will testify about me" (John 15:26). This Spirit of truth "will guide you into all truth" and will "tell you what is yet to come" (John 16:13). However, to engage fully His resources, we must be "led by the Spirit" (Romans 8:14), "live by the Spirit" (Galatians 5:16), "keep in step with the Spirit" (Galatians 5:25), not "grieve" or "quench" the Spirit (Ephesians 4:30; 1 Thessalonians 5:19), and "be filled with the Spirit" (Ephesians 5:18).

Since Satan is a counterfeiter rather than a creator, one of his ploys is bogus spiritual manifestations. He orchestrates events and demonstrations that purport to be God's doings. He motivates people to speak what they claim are the words of God. By circulating his fake spiritual currency, the deceiver tries to destabilize God's economy.

Thus an invaluable tool is spiritual discernment, the "balance wheel" of the spiritual gifts. It provides supernatural enabling to distinguish between the true and false, between the hand of God and the sleight-of-hand of the devil. It serves as the Church's precious metal detector to discern the difference between gold and pyrite, or "fool's" gold.

Three Sources

Spiritual manifestations stem from three basic sources: the divine, the demonic, and the human. Some folks assume that everything originates either from God or the devil. Yet many manifestations and ministries are neither divine nor demonic. They are either entirely human in origin, or they combine the human with either the divine or demonic. Like either black or white paint mixed with green, they create a color all their own. I've seen things I don't think either God or Satan would want to claim. What occurred was just fallible, faulty human nature at work.

God is infallible. His Word is infallible. However, human behavior isn't. "We have this treasure in jars of clay" (2 Corinthians 4:7), so don't mistake the pot for the prize. Spiritual expressions such as words of knowledge, gifts of tongues, and miraculous powers can be confused, misused, and abused. Don't ever put a word of prophecy or interpretation of tongues on the same level as the Bible. Rather, measure their worth *by* the Bible.

Human spirits, still bearing traces of the *imago dei*, often mimic the manifestations of the Holy One. In the Church you'll find a variety of these fleshly fakes. Such as the spirit of tradition, which does obeisance to the past and attempts to duplicate that "old-time religion" for every succeeding generation. Or the spirits of compassion and pity, well-intentioned saints anxious to see every sick person miraculously healed and every worship service more sensational than the last. Or the spirit of envy. The spirit of pride. The spirit of divisiveness.

Sometimes these spiritual misfires are amusing. A woman in one church had been controlling the congregation with her "fireworks." When an evangelist began to preach things that threatened her stranglehold—or, stronghold—she responded by prophesying. Several times she interrupted services by jumping up to give "a word from the Lord."

Finally the evangelist had had enough. "Madam," he reprimanded her from the pulpit, "will you please sit down and keep quiet." She obeyed, but not for long. With further weapons in her arsenal, she soon leaped to her feet.

"Yea," she bellowed (in King James English, of course), "thus saith the Lord: 'thou dost think thou art a humdinger; but, thus saith the Lord, thou art not a humdinger.'"

A gentleman offered this revealing "message" in a service: "Thus saith the Lord, 'My little children, I know you're scared. But don't you worry. Sometimes I get scared Myself.'" (Now that *is* scary.)

A fellow in another church, noted for his attention-getting tactics, rose one night to proclaim, "Thus saith the Lord, 'When I zig, you zag. And when I zag, you zig. I'm confused,' saith the Lord."

You don't have to be one of the original apostles to figure out these messages didn't carry God's personal signature. Of course, not all mani*flesh*tations are that extreme or obvious. The point is that, whenever human beings are involved, the potential for error exists. Even the most mature and respected believer can mix self in with the Spirit and distort His workings. Fool's gold spills in with the real gold, and an expert eye is required to spot the difference.

Test the Spirits

So the Bible urges us to "test the spirits." Both 1 John 4:1 and 1 Thessalonians 5:21 use *dokimadzo*, a term that means to test or to prove. For us it conjures up an image like those quality control inspectors. To first-century dwellers, the word brought to mind those who dealt in precious metals and tested them to verify their genuineness.

Therefore the meaning is usually positive: "test in order to approve." Spiritual discernment isn't given to allow us to pick out every fault and flaw in people's lives but to enable us to determine whether something is God's bona fide doing. "Test everything," Paul instructs. "Hold on to the good." Then he adds, "Avoid every kind of evil."

"The operation of the spirit of discernment," observes Kenneth Kinghorn (*Gifts of the Spirit*, Abingdon, 1976), "will give approval to teaching and preaching that brings fresh truth from God. In the Church we need to concentrate on the pluses more than the minuses."

Some Christians see themselves as counterfeit experts, and conceive their mission to be ferreting out everything phony (which they think is almost everybody and everything except themselves). The danger of going after every weed, Jesus cautioned (Matthew 13:24-30), is you're likely to yank up wheat along with it. Besides, the best way to recognize the fake is to become thoroughly familiar with the authentic. Keep your eyes *out* for the devil but keep your eyes *on* Jesus.

Following the Civil War, Elijah McCoy, the son of runaway slaves, moved to Michigan to work for the railroad. There he invented the automatic lubricator which revolutionized the operation of the steam locomotive. Others attempted to copy his work, but railroad workers didn't like the other versions and demanded "the real McCoy." God wants us focused on the authentic.

If the genuine exists, however, imitations will surely surface. Use of the phrase, "every spirit" (1 John 4:1), reminds us that a multitude of them are out there, "and many false prophets have gone out" to wreak havoc and deception on the Church. To detect the fraudulent requires special equipment—the discernment of the Holy Spirit. And while this discernment is a supernatural gifting, several practical principles mark the path we should follow.

Five Tests

Five basic tests help us validate God's workings.

1) ***Truth Test.*** The truth test simply measures whether a message proves accurate. If someone prophesies that something will happen, it will if the prophecy is valid. If it doesn't occur, then the statement didn't originate with God. The speaker may have been sincere. Nevertheless, he/she was sincerely wrong.

"If what a prophet proclaims in the name of the Lord does not take place or come true, that is a message the Lord has not spoken. The prophet has spoken presumptuously. Do not be afraid of him" (Deuteronomy 18:22).

In one congregation, a lady prophesied that a sister member would be miraculously healed and raised up to a new ministry in years to come. It felt good and sounded good. Everyone in the building yearned for it to happen. Afterward the pastor gushed, "We have been to the mountain, the Lord has spoken, and this woman is going to get well." Six weeks later they conducted her funeral in that same sanctuary. The church felt devastated. They had mistaken good news for God's news.

2) ***Word Test.*** This exam gauges whether words or actions harmonize with the Bible. Christians can save themselves so much heartache by knowing the Scriptures well. Dr. Culbreth Melton of Emmanuel College has given a practical but classic message on finding God's will. One thing he tells students is that 95 percent of God's will is already spelled out in the Bible, and if they'll become well-versed in that, they will identify the other five percent much more easily.

We are to judge *everything* by the Book. It is foolproof and will keep us from making fools of ourselves. Ask yourself whether a ministry or manifestation mirrors what the Bible says about Christ. "Every spirit that acknowledges that Jesus Christ has come in the flesh is from God, but every spirit that does not acknowledge Jesus is not from God. This is the spirit of the antichrist ..." (1 John 4:2, 3).

Ask whether the teacher and teaching mesh with what the Bible says about salvation. "Even if we or an angel from heaven should preach a gospel other than the one we preached to you, let him be eternally condemned!" Paul exclaims, then repeats himself to make sure the severity of his words sink in.

Ask whether the word or wonder complements or contradicts God's commandments. "If a prophet, or one who foretells by dreams, appears among you and announces to you a miraculous sign or wonder, and if the sign or wonder of which he has spoken takes place, and he says, 'Let us follow other gods' (gods you have not known) 'and let us worship them,' you must not listen to the words of that prophet or dreamer .... It is the Lord your God you must follow, and him you must revere. Keep his commands and obey him; serve him and hold fast to him" (Deuteronomy 13:1-4).

No matter how magnificent the miracle, no matter how marvelous the message, no matter how mesmerizing the minister, if it contradicts the Word of God, trash it. Toss it out like you would trash spoiled meat.

A man and woman wanted to get married. In fact, they told a minister that God had told them to marry. Sounds very spiritual, doesn't it? One tiny hurdle remained: each was already married to someone else. That pastor didn't need to pray for guidance or seek others' counsel. In this situation, God's will was already on paper. "We can easily psyche ourselves past God's already-revealed will in order to do what we want," Dr. Melton observes.

That becomes easier when we understand the Bible poorly, or when we swallow the far-out theology of the latest spiritual huckster. When every street corner of the Church seems to contain another preacher pushing some junk food teaching that claims to revolutionize people's lives (especially if they'll send money), we need a steady diet of the meat-and-potatoes truths of God's Word.

Beware of "Lone Ranger" prophets and teachers. A test which came to be applied during the Montanist heresy of the second century was "the willingness to submit to Church leadership, and to allow Scripture to be decisive. God is not the author of confusion, and he is not the source of any teaching through a so-called prophet which conflicts with the apostolic testimony about Jesus, nor with duly appointed leadership loyal to that standard" (Michael Green, *I Believe in the Holy Spirit*, Eerdmans, 1975).

3) ***Spirit Test.*** The Spirit test is furnished by the Holy Spirit who lives in each believer as well as the corporate body of Christ. In tandem with the Word, the Spirit validates that which is authentic and steers us skillfully away from the hidden, jagged rocks of excess and error. "Every spirit that does not acknowledge Jesus is not from God. This is the spirit of the antichrist ... You, dear children, are from God and have overcome them, because the one who is in you is greater than the one who is in the world ... This is how we recognize the Spirit of truth and the spirit of falsehood" (1 John 4:3-6).

Every Christian needs to learn to recognize the Spirit's voice. To listen to Him and move with Him. "Do not put out the Spirit's fire," cautions the apostle Paul (1 Thessalonians 5:19). Or as other translations put it, don't "quench," "suppress" or "smother" the Holy Spirit. How can we distinguish between genuine and counterfeit expressions when we aren't tuned in to the genuine? And how can we free the Spirit to work if we're so fearful of the false that we pour water on every spark of fire He kindles?

Evaluate what's taking place with these questions.

—Does it harmonize with the Holy Spirit's nature?

—Does the Spirit of Christ shine through it?

—Are the fruits of the Spirit evident in it?

—Does it fit the Spirit's pattern of operation?

Knowing the Bible's teaching on the third Person of the Godhead will help you apply these accurately.

Jesus said, "I have come to bring fire on the earth" (Luke 12:49), and that imperishable inferno, the Spirit of truth, is kindling incredible blazes. Satan's rats nests are being scorched around the globe. Every week 70,000 sinners come to Christ and 3,500 new churches are built. Don't let the spirits of error scare you away. Catch the wave. Fan the flame.

4) ***Grace Test.*** The grace test examines the result of a ministry or manifestation. Does it put people in bondage or bring freedom? Build up Christ's body or tear it down? Create hope or despair? Open the door for us to "approach the throne of grace with confidence" (Hebrews 4:16), or slam the door in our faces?

Demonic spirits always seek to put believers back in bondage. "The Spirit clearly says that in later times some will abandon the faith and follow deceiving spirits and things taught by demons ... They forbid people to marry and order them to abstain from certain foods, which God created to be received with thanksgiving" (1 Timothy 4:1-3). "See to it that no one takes you captive through hollow and deceptive philosophy, which depends on human tradition and the basic principles of the world rather than on Christ" (Colossians 2:8). "Now that you know God—or rather are known by God—how is it that you are turning back to those weak and miserable principles? Do you wish to be enslaved by them all over again?" (Galatians 4:9).

On the contrary, the Spirit liberates people. "When God is personally present, a living Spirit, that old, constricting legislation is recognized as obsolete. We're free of it! All of us! Nothing between us and God, our faces shining with the brightness of his face. And so we are transfigured much like the Messiah, our lives gradually becoming brighter and more beautiful as God enters our lives and we become like him" (2 Corinthians 3:17, 18, Peterson).

5) ***Glory Test.*** Who gets the credit for what happens? Who is honored? The glory test performs a credit check on ministry

words and behaviors. When humans, who are only "clay pot" instruments through which God works, get primary glory, then demonic and/or human spirits have been at work. When the spotlight shines on Christ, then the Spirit of the Lord is behind it.

The Holy Spirit *always* seeks to glorify Jesus Christ. "The Counselor, the Holy Spirit, whom the Father will send in my name, will teach you all things and will remind you of everything I have said to you" (John 14:26). "He will guide you into all truth. He will not speak on his own; he will speak only what he hears, and he will tell you what is yet to come. He will bring glory to me by taking from what is mine and making it known to you" (John 16:13, 14).

We live in a "glory" culture where fame is often the ultimate high. Even many Christians fall into the hero-worshipping trap, and high-profile ministers and ministries sometimes receive the adulation of rock stars. The focus easily turns from "How great Thou art!" to "How great I am!" We stop marching to Gabriel's trumpet and start honking our own. Don't ever forget: grabbing God's glory for himself was the devil's downfall. Applying the glory test more rigorously would save the body of Christ tremendous pain and embarrassment.

The Nuts and Bolts

When do we exercise the gift of discernment? Under what circumstances is it to be used? *When a "word" from the Lord or a manifestation of power takes place, or when someone claims to be speaking or acting on behalf of God.* This Spirit-charged perception isn't an X-ray that tells whether a person is a Christian or reveals his/her innermost secrets. Rather it functions as a litmus test of what is authentically the Spirit's doing in the Church's worship and ministry.

Why is it necessary? *To prevent confusion and false teaching* *from infiltrating the Church.* It guards God's people from the deception of Satan, who often presents himself as an angel of light. Discernment also helps restrain human spirits from "getting into the flesh" with imitation manifestations.

Who exercises this gift? Some believe the gift of discernment operates regularly in certain persons, while others think it functions spontaneously in various individuals as the need arises. *To some extent it involves the whole Church in testing words and actions that are presented before the body. However, the leaders—pastors, elders, etc.—bear primary responsibility.* That's why it's often important for church members to test a prophecy or idea with their leaders before sharing it publicly. Ultimately the shepherds must protect the flock from bogus spirituality, even if that means disappointing or angering overeager individuals.

How should it be done? *Wisely. Lovingly. As gently as the circumstances allow, yet as firmly as needed to protect the body and give clear direction.* "Everything should be done in a fitting and orderly way" (1 Corinthians 15:40), including the distinguishing of spirits. A well-intentioned but faulty human response warrants a softer touch than a demonically-orchestrated charade. Sometimes validation or invalidation needs to take place publicly and immediately to prevent the congregation's being misled. On other occasions, the situation is best dealt with later, either privately or by subsequent public instruction. The intent is always to approve the genuine God-given phenomenon, while protecting believers from confusion and deception. Discerning of spirits is intended to be an affirming, healing ministry of and to the Church.

Police estimated the odds as "a million to one." In Sheboygan, Wisconsin, on the same day several years ago, two men named Baker each drove his 1978 maroon AMC Concord to Northgate Shopping Center. When Richard Baker and his wife finished their shopping, they returned to the car and drove off. As they drove home from a later errand, she noticed a strange pair of sunglasses. "Whose are these?" she asked. Examining the automobile more carefully, they noticed several things that weren't right. A check of the tags confirmed their fears. "This isn't our car!"

They raced back to the Northgate parking lot to find policemen with a Thomas Baker, who had reported his car stolen. It took some explaining, but when Richard Baker convinced the police to try the keys, both men's keys unlocked and operated both vehicles. Here were two cars so much alike that only subtle differences differentiated one from the other.

It happened on April Fool's Day.

In spiritual warfare, the odds are much smaller than a million to one. Other spirits than the Holy Spirit vie for recognition and legitimacy. They mimic His workings to the smallest detail. To the casual observer, they look the same and operate the same. Discerning believers, however, will notice that something isn't quite right.

Don't be fooled by "seconds" or imitations, heaven's quality control warns us.

Accept only the real McCoy.

We can easily forgive a child who is afraid of the dark; the real tragedy of life is when men are afraid of the light.

—Plato

It is of no advantage to be near the light if the eyes are closed.

—Augustine

Many Christians define sin as the sum total of acts which they themselves do not commit.

—Carlyle Marney

10

Pharisaism— The Devil's Religion

The nation of France folded to the Germans early in World War II, their army impotent against the Nazi might. By June 1940 German troops occupied Paris. The French were a conquered people. Masses of citizens decided to make the best of a bad situation and cooperate.

Others refused to give in, however. Organized as an "underground army," the French resistance constantly nipped at its captor's heels. Their guerrilla warfare damaged Germany's war effort, dynamiting roads and bridges, stealing military secrets, and smuggling people and goods.

The devil is a guerrilla fighter. While he recognizes that he's no match for God in a straight-up battle, he tries to damage God's kingdom and slow its advance through subversion and confusion. One way he does so is by turning Christianity into grotesque distortions of itself. However he can infiltrate the King's organization and distort or disrupt it, he will. He had a game plan he used when Jesus came, and his tactics today look much the same.

At just the right time, the Holy One came in the flesh. God Himself invaded planet earth with the purpose of founding the Church as a supernatural organism of divine deliverance. Satan countered with a two-pronged, underground resistance. Both prongs were religious weapons. He wanted to undermine God's forces through sabotage by their own kind.

Jesus saw what the evil one was up to (or down to), but He had trouble getting His subordinates to understand. "Be careful," He cautioned them one day as their boat bobbed across the lake (Matthew 16). "Be on your guard against the yeast of the Pharisees and Sadducees."

His disciples quickly conferred, baffled once again by the Master's words. "It is because we didn't bring any bread," they finally concluded.

Exasperated, the Lord responded, "You of little faith, why are you talking among yourselves about having no bread?" Reminding them of His two miraculous feedings of crowds, He continued, "How is it you don't understand that I was not talking to you about bread? But be on your guard against the yeast of the Pharisees and Sadducees." Finally it dawned on them that Jesus was warning them of the teachings of the two groups.

The context for this incident is *launching*: God launching his concluding mission in our world. The mystery of the

Church is the greatest mystery of God's divine revelation. Following their boat ride, the Son of God talked about His plan, promising that He would build the Church and make it triumphant. Victorious. Unbeatable. Not even the gates of hell could withstand its advance. It would achieve everything God had designed for it to achieve.

Along the way, however, Satan has tried to frustrate, divert, destroy, cripple God's master plan. Chapter 8 explains one way that the dark prince attempts to subvert the Church. He constructs strongholds in people's minds which prevent them from thinking God's thoughts and seeing reality from His perspective. Chapter 9 shows another—counterfeiting the Spirit's working. Yet another tool the dark one uses is the "yeast" of Sadducees and Pharisees. He creates deformed and despicable caricatures of the faith to contaminate the living bread.

Two Poisons

In Jesus' day, in that seedbed of Judaism from which sprouted the Messiah and the Church, two predominant religious groups existed, antithetical to each other and holding opposite views of Scripture. Both groups professed to follow Jehovah, and both saw themselves as true Israelites. They had the name and made the claim.

Ironically, these two sects made up the primary opposition to Jesus' earthly ministry. They also led the effort to abort the infant Church. Paul had a running battle with the Judaizers throughout his ministry.

In the lake-crossing dialogue Jesus spoke sternly. "I'm warning you against the leaven both of the Pharisees and the Sadducees. If you're going to be my instruments to bring God's kingdom into place, you must keep these two brands of poison out of the Church."

Neither the Pharisees nor Sadducees could ever see what

God was up to. They blinded themselves to the truth. Even when the Light shone all around them, they refused to open their eyes. They weren't where the action was and didn't want to be. In fact, they refused to believe Jesus' miracles and teachings were of God. They branded the Son of Man as demonic. They buttressed their views with exhaustive theological arguments from their labyrinthine and esoteric theology (like some people insulate themselves against the truth today).

Yet the Pharisees and Sadducees were polar opposites. Antagonism to the Messiah was about the only thing they agreed on. In fact, one thing that convinced the Sadducees their beliefs were right was how different they were from the Pharisees. The Sadducees saw themselves as modern and enlightened in contrast to their old fogy counterparts. Conversely, the Pharisees were convinced they were the spiritually correct ones, while the Sadducees were backslidden apostates. Fundamentalists versus liberals, you might describe it.

How opposed the two sects were is graphically seen in Acts 23. Called before a hostile Sanhedrin, Paul started talking about the resurrection. That quickly turned the meeting into a brouhaha between the two groups, because the Sadducees didn't believe in the resurrection while the Pharisees did.

Interestingly, Jesus didn't have nearly as much trouble with the Sadducees, whom He dismissed rather quickly and easily, as He did their legalistic opponents. The Pharisees, however, harassed and hounded Him constantly, and their orthodox standing made them a formidable foe.

The Sadducees had abandoned faith in the resurrection. They reasoned that the current life was all there was. Nor did they believe in angels, demons, or anything supernatural. They were the humanists, the rationalists of their time. Like modern theological liberalism, they only accepted parts of the Bible. They embraced only the first five books, and they had edited those. Therefore they were closed to anything supernatural about the ministry of Jesus, and they constantly haggled over inconsequential things (such as their conundrum about the wife and her seven husbands, Luke 20: 27-38). With X-ray clarity, the Master exposed their two fatal flaws: "You know neither the Scriptures nor the power of God."

Doesn't that aptly depict Liberalism? Sadducean Christianity is like a shiny, expensive car with no engine. It looks nice and is a respectable thing to have sitting in your driveway, but it lacks the power to take you anywhere. Modernism has been devastating to Christ's cause by allowing people to reject basic gospel realities while still thinking they're on the right road toward God.

Piety Gone Sour

Pharisees, however, are a different breed. They have been and are the cancer in conservative Christianity. In Christ's time they were the biblical specialists. They knew the Word of God inside and out and had dedicated their whole lives to studying Scripture. Sadly, they studied for the wrong reason: so they could club others over the head.

The Pharisees had become experts at binding people up and burdening them down. They produced rules and regulations for every possible situation, but the machinery of restriction was not lubricated by the oil of compassion. Every minute detail was forged into yet another link in an immense chain that shackled thirsty souls.

The most blistering words Christ ever spoke were targeted at these storm troopers of legalism. He fired indictments like these: "The teachers of the law and Pharisees sit in Moses' seat. So you must obey them and do everything they tell you. But do not do what they do, for they do not practice what they preach. They tie up heavy loads and put them on men's shoulders, but they themselves are not willing to lift a finger to move them" (Matthew 23:2-4).

The Master ripped their externalism. "Everything they do is done for men to see" (23:5). He exposed their love for the spotlight, titles, awards, and adulation. In return, they hated Him for refusing to dance to their human traditions. It infuriated them to hear Him say that what was on the outside of a person didn't matter, but what came from within.

It angered them because it was true: "Woe to you, teachers of the law and Pharisees, you hypocrites! You clean the outside of the cup and dish, but inside they are full of greed and self-indulgence ... You are like whitewashed tombs, which look beautiful on the outside but on the inside are full of dead men's bones and everything unclean" (Matthew 23:25-27).

I learned early in my ministry—learned it the hard way—that legalists are often covering up their own sins. As a young pastor I encountered church members who came down hard on everybody else as a cover-up for their own misdeeds. They were covering themselves, and perhaps reacting to their stricken consciences by pointing fingers at everyone else.

Like security guards in an airport concourse, these Pharisees blocked the doors to the kingdom. They were determined not to let anyone through who didn't fit exactly their stereotypes. Their "mettle" detectors would shriek at the smallest hint of irregularity. They slammed the kingdom gates in men's faces. "They themselves will not enter, nor will they let those enter who are trying to" (23:13).

Herein lies a great tragedy of Pharisaism in any age. Those who obscure God's reality never harm themselves alone. They leave strewn along their self-righteous trail lots of spiritual corpses, genuine seekers destroyed or disillusioned after being roughed up by these hypocrites. The victory, the deliverance God would like to bring to so many people never gets through because of pseudo-saints who jam His gospel signals with static. By the time they get through with it, the truth looks like one of those scrambled pay-TV pictures: ugly and unintelligible.

Christian Lookalikes

One of the problems with Pharisees, then and now, is that they appear so kosher. Pharisees are often the most loyal church members. They hardly ever miss a service. They're usually among the biggest givers. They gladly take positions of responsibility, and they seem the most clean-living, respectable people in town—solid as a rock. They look right, act right, even smell right. However, that's one reason why they do so much damage. It's hard to budge a "pillar of the faith."

On the surface the Pharisees of the New Testament seemed admirable. They were evangelistic (though for the wrong reasons). "You travel over land and sea to win a single convert and when he becomes one, you make him twice as much a son of hell as you are" (23:15). That's why legalism is as hard to exterminate as roaches from a third-rate motel. Pharisees aggressively reproduce themselves, partly because they can't be satisfied until everyone else is exactly like they are.

They were also scripturalists. They believed the Bible. Every word, every letter. They'd fight you over the authority of Scripture. They believed their Bible. Of course, that was the problem: they believed *their* Bible. The way they interpreted the Law and Prophets was to them the only right way.

And they were ardent givers. They paid tithes on everything, even their herb gardens. They were scrupulous in other areas too. That's one reason there were only a few thousand of them in Jesus' time. You had to be pretty smart just to memorize all the rules, let alone keep them. Their regulations covered whom you could eat with and work with, where you could go, what you could wear, what you could eat. Every square inch of one's life was controlled by restrictions.

For instance, if an insect was biting a Pharisee on the Sabbath, he could not kill it or he would be breaking the law against hunting. And if he were to spit, it must be on a rock, for to spit on the ground would part the dirt and make one guilty of plowing.

But they weren't satisfied to be dogmatic and hidebound themselves. They dogged everybody else's hide also. The Pharisees persecuted those who saw things differently. Therefore they attacked Jesus with a vengeance, for He violated all their rules. They called Him a glutton, a drunkard, a liar, and demon-possessed, among other things. On His part, He seemed to look for an opportunity to pick a fight with them. The Master perfectly obeyed all of God's Law, but He refused to be bound by the manmade traditions of the Pharisees. He didn't tiptoe around their hatefulness to keep the peace.

God's Murderers

How they hated Christ. Ultimately they pulled enough strings to get Him crucified, and they regretted only that they couldn't have pulled it off sooner. They had Him killed because He was getting in their way. He didn't fit into their tight little boxes. They despised His flouting of their laws, His constant mingling with the irreligious, and His working of miracles. Their belief in Scripture was past tense; God wasn't in the miracle business any longer. Therefore this traveling Teacher who did signs and wonders and flouted their rules must be apostate.

For all their knowledge and piety, the Pharisees were blind as tree trunks to the truth. In spite of their dedication to the Word, when the Word showed up in the flesh, they had no idea whom they were looking at. These religious giants who had devoted their whole lives to following God didn't have a clue as to what God was up to. They missed the boat so badly that the Savior once ruefully observed, "The tax collectors and the prostitutes are entering the kingdom of God ahead of you" (Matthew 21:31). Ouch!

Does that unnerve you? It's a warning of the blinding, suffocating tendencies of spirituality in human hands. The greatest enemy of the Church often is the Church. The devil infiltrates our own army and uses it against us. These first-century hypocrites took the greatest reality in the universe—the truth about God—and twisted it until it was unrecognizable. The Creator and Sustainer of all had come to earth and stood inches away from their faces, and all they wanted to do was murder Him.

Talk about granite hearts. Jesus had once told the parable of the rich man and Lazarus, in which the rich man pleads for Lazarus to return from the dead because surely a resurrected corpse would convince the man's five brothers. Yet when a real-life Lazarus walked from the grave, the Sanhedrin decided they must kill both Jesus and him.

Stephen later hit the bull's eye with his scathing rebuke in Acts 7: "You stiff-necked people, with uncircumcised hearts and ears! You are just like your fathers: You always resist the Holy Spirit. Was there ever a prophet your fathers did not persecute? They even killed those who predicted the coming of the Righteous One. And now you have betrayed and murdered him" (vv. 51, 52). Obviously Stephen's speech deeply moved them, for they offed him too, before he could even finish his sermon and give the invitation.

Can you understand why Christ spoke so brutally to and about them? He never talked anywhere nearly that harshly to anyone else, not even the worst sinner. But the Pharisees and scribes He called hypocrites. Snakes. Blind guides. Whitewashed tombs. Murderers. "You belong to your father, the devil, and you want to carry out your father's desire. He was a murderer from the beginning, not holding to the truth, for there is no truth in him" (John 8:44).

We should learn an important lesson here. The Church has suffered entirely too much from Pharisaism. We have been quick to tackle the adulterer and the heretic, but slow to confront those who condemn and control and crush the Church's influence in the community by their harsh and hateful behavior. We ought to take a cue from Jesus and be more confrontive of those who do the devil's dirty work right in the house of God.

No, we aren't to be pharisaic with Pharisees. Despite Christ's bluntness, He still wept over their hard hearts (23:37). While He blasted their ways, He grieved for their souls (Mark 2:5). However, the Church needs to deal ruthlessly with the "leaven" that penetrates and poisons its effectiveness. Pharisaism is nothing less than the devil's religion, an insidious weapon the archfiend uses to fight God's kingdom plan.

We must also deal firmly with the Pharisaism we find in our own hearts. The yeast of the Pharisees is not an all-or-nothing proposition. Many otherwise solid believers retain pockets of legalism. Some folks shucked their legalistic cloak and lists of rules years ago, but their hearts still possess a rigidity that resists the Spirit's free reign. Even someone as godly and full of the Spirit as Peter, who had experienced that amazing vision opening his heart to the Gentiles, experienced an occasional relapse. Paul had to get in his face and shake him back to gospel reality (Galatians 2:11-21).

Still Among Us

Sadly, not all the Pharisees died in the first century. Their evangelistic methods have proved effective. Their sanctimonious successors are still among us. They still have their rules. They still condemn those around them. They still use the

Bible as a billy-club to subdue the Church to their wills. They still block hungry souls from spiritual reality. They still live in the past, blind to the new wineskins into which God is pouring His Spirit.

The Mighty One is active today. He's working miracles. He's reaching the "tax collectors and prostitutes," the outcasts and rejects, with the Good News. He's building His Church and tearing down walls of demonic opposition. Emmanuel is with us, but Pharisees can't see the forest for the trees.

Some of us find ourselves today in the same situation as the first century. We're so "spiritually correct" we think we have it all figured out. We know what's orthodox and what isn't. How God works and how He doesn't. We're experts in the Law. Yet if Jesus came in the flesh today, we probably wouldn't recognize or accept Him any more than the ultra religious did 20 centuries ago.

A colleague became senior pastor of a large congregation. When he was hired, they told him they wanted to grow and to reach the lost. So after he'd been there a year, he began preaching about the Father's passion for the prodigal and the dangers of the "older brother syndrome." Soon a sizable element of the members began agitating for his dismissal. They accused him of unbiblical preaching, of lack of respect for church traditions, of befriending the wrong kind of people ("persons who don't fit in with this church"). His pastorate lasted two years.

Does this sound familiar? It should. It happens often.

What about you? If God began a revolutionary work in your congregation, would you endorse it? If lost people from different backgrounds than your present membership came to Christ, how would you treat them? If drug addicts and alcoholics and ex-cons and homosexuals experienced transformation, would you feel thrilled or threatened? If persons who don't talk like you or dress like you showed up for church, what would it do to the celebration of worship? And if they got in the door, what kinds of hoops would you make them jump through before you gave your stamp of approval?

A major difference between true religion and Pharisaism is its effects on its adherents. Pharisaism puts people in a strait jacket. Genuine Christianity liberates them. The Spirit of the Lord is the Spirit of freedom. "It has been decided by the Holy Spirit and by ourselves," the Jerusalem council wrote the Gentile churches (Acts 15), "not to saddle you with any burden beyond these essentials ...." Is the ministry of your congregation saddling people with heavy loads or setting them free?

Some congregations are sinking like the Titanic because their pastors and leaders have been loading them down with so much "stuff." If instead they would just give their people the Word of God, give them Jesus Christ and turn Him loose in their lives, those churches might explode with renewal. Christ accepts people where they are and then leads them by His Spirit to where they need to go.

"Don't let the ways of the Pharisees and Sadducees contaminate My Church," Jesus pleaded with His lieutenants. "Their yeast will ruin the bread of life so that it's not fit to feed starving sinners. Keep this poison out!"

God is doing incredible things in our world today. We don't need to worry about His Church. It's invincible against even the gates of hell. Our concern had better be whether we're moving in the swift, deep current of God's Spirit or mucking things up near the shore.

Harold Presley, a pastor in London, England, recalls boyhood days swimming with his brother and cousins in a wide pool in a south Alabama creek. Harold's younger brother Pete was only four and afraid of the deeper, darker water. However, he was fascinated by the colored pebbles in the shallows and would tromp around, collecting more than he could ever take home.

He also stirred up a great deal of mud, and in the shallow water it was not swept away by the current as quickly as in the deeper part of the swimming hole. Finally, Harold would yell, "Peter John, either get all the way in, or get all the way out! You're ruining the swimming for the rest of us."

Are we swimmers or collectors? Are we moving with the Spirit or muddying up the water?

I want to get all the way into the stream of God's workings. Don't you?

[Jesus] rose up from the place where the kingdoms of the world shimmered before him, where crowns flashed and banners rustled, and hosts of enthusiastic people were ready to acclaim him, and quietly walked the way of poverty and suffering to the cross

—Helmut Thielicke

I've heard a lot of sermons in the past 10 years or so that make me want to get up and walk out. They're secular, psychological, self-help sermons. Friendly, but of no use. They didn't make you straighten up. They didn't give you anything hard .... At some point and in some way, a sermon has to direct people toward the death of Christ and the campaign that God has waged over the centuries to get our attention.

—Garrison Keillor

11

Communion of Conquerors

Ted Turner, media mogul, declared to a group of broadcasters a few years ago, "Christianity is for losers." Sorry, Ted, but you are dead wrong. Christianity is for winners. In spite of the fact that the theme song of some

Christians seems to be "Born to Lose," the Word of God says that we are "more than conquerors."

Of all the books of the Bible, the last one seems the most complex and puzzling. Revelation is shrouded in mist and painted with deep shadows. Some of its content, written in an apocalyptic style familiar to its ancient readers, is foreign to modern ears.

Nevertheless, whatever your interpretive approach to the apostle John's vision, you can hardly mistake the meaning of chapter 12. The identity of the principal characters is evident: the woman (Israel), the male child (Jesus), the dragon (Satan), the stars (those angels which fell with him). Just as clear is the message: the devil and his legions are defeated—hurled down to the earth. For all practical purposes the war is over. The rest of Revelation chronicles the wipe-up campaign, but the final outcome from here on is etched in stone.

Amid this pivotal scene rings a powerful voice out of heaven, an angelic messenger with a declaration regarding the victory of God's people. "The saints have overcome," he announces. "Their accuser has been crushed, and they are eternally victorious." Not stopping there, the angel goes on to tell how God's soldiers won, what their three secret weapons were. "They overcame him by the blood of the Lamb and by the word of their testimony; they did not love their lives so much as to shrink from death. Therefore rejoice..." (12:11, 12).

These words are familiar, often quoted among Christians. Unfortunately, the angel's statement is frequently used with so little understanding that it is pregnant with meaning for the victorious believer.

In fact, many of us who've grown up in the church have tossed around a number of biblical phrases until they're threadbare, none more so than "the blood of the Lamb." We glibly sing and preach about the blood of the Lamb as though it were some spiritual Pine Sol®, handily available whenever we need to cleanse away a few annoying spots. We're prone to give little thought to the awesome circumstances wherein that blood was shed.

God's Little Lamb

The words of Revelation 12:11 refer to nothing less than the death of Jesus, the Passover Lamb. In fact, the Lamb of God is the central character of Revelation. In chapter 7, those who've come out of the great tribulation wash their robes in His blood. In chapter 13, He's described as "slain from the creation of the world." Those who've won victory over the beast sing "the song of the Lamb" in chapter 15. The Lamb is depicted in chapter 17 as "King of kings and Lord of lords." Chapter 19 portrays the wedding of the Lamb. The Lamb's book of life and throne are part of the New Jerusalem scene in chapters 21 and 22, and He serves both as temple and light for the city. In other places, the book employs kindred descriptions such as "him whom they pierced," "who died and came to life again," "he has freed us by his blood," and "he is dressed in a robe dipped in blood."

However, the first (and perhaps most notable) Lamb reference is found in chapter 5. There the title deed to our inheritance is being held in the right hand of the One sitting on the throne. When an angel cries out, "Who is worthy to break the seals and open the scroll?" it appears at first that no one anywhere is qualified. John sobs until one of the elders around the throne calls out, "Do not weep! See, the Lion of the tribe of Judah, the Root of David, has triumphed. He is able to open the scroll and its seven seals."

When John turns to look, however, he sees not a Lion but a Lamb, "looking as if it had been slain." That bloodied Lamb is the basis for all the hopes of the righteous multitude, and at His appearance a tremendous celebration breaks out. "You are worthy to take the scroll and open its seals, because you were slain, and with your blood you purchased men for God from every tribe and language and people and nation."

This scene carries the observer back to Exodus 12. There the children of Israel, in bondage for four centuries, stand on the threshold of freedom. God has promised to bring them out of Egypt into a land of hope, a land oozing with blessings. Yet to the Israelites it seems like fantasy-land. The tension builds as the Lord raises the ante, plague by plague, while the Egyptians stubbornly hold out. The Mighty One always delivers on His promises, however, and with one final plague He will both land the crushing blow and teach His people the most important lesson they'll ever learn. It is a kindergarten lesson in salvation.

"This is a day you are to remember as long as you're a nation," God instructs Moses and Aaron. "Every year for the generations to come you shall celebrate it as a festival to the Lord." With that Yahweh gives His people specific directions for observing what will become their most hallowed festival, the Passover.

Each family is to select a lamb less than one year old, one without any defects or disease, and bring it into the household to live with the family members for four days. Then they are to take that innocent, helpless creature, to whom they've become attached, and slit its throat. Its blood is to be smeared on the door frame and its flesh is to be roasted and eaten. Then, when the angel of death brings the tenth and most horrible plague on the nation of Egypt—the death of every firstborn child—the blood-marked Israelite homes will be spared.

A day to remember? How could they ever forget that incredible moment when their God struck down their powerful captors? When every household from Pharaoh's on down lost a son? When the stench of death and the wails of grief overpowered the country? When incredibly the Hebrews suffered no loss of life among their own—not even a cow or goat? When they received their traveling papers and trekked out of a place in which they all had been sure they'd die?

Saved by the blood of a lamb! Though they couldn't fully comprehend its meaning, its message was indelibly burned into their brains. From the sacrifices of Leviticus to the mute sheep of Isaiah 53, that image would dominate the national consciousness.

The identity of God's Passover Lamb is accented by the word used for "lamb" throughout the Book of Revelation. John does not use the common word for lamb, but the Greek word meaning "little pet lamb." It refers without question to the perennial little pet lamb sharply etched in the minds of every true child of Israel.

Secret Weapon #1—Stand on the Blood

Now fast forward a millennium-and-a-half. A rough-hewn fellow named John is baptizing penitents in a muddy river. Suddenly he spots Jesus, apparently unknown to the crowds, walking toward him. What words do you think burst from John's lips? "Look, the Lamb of God who takes away the sin of the world!" John's prophetic outburst sends a shiver down the spine. This time God is providing the Lamb, and it's *His* firstborn Son. A far bigger Egypt will fall with this sacrifice. No wonder the Christmas carol muses about the Savior's birth, "The hopes and fears of all the years are met in Thee tonight."

The apostle Paul, glimpsing later somewhat the same sight John the Baptist did, proclaims those classic words, "I consider everything a loss compared to the surpassing greatness of knowing Christ Jesus my Lord, for whose sake I have lost all things. I consider them rubbish that I may gain Christ and be found in him, not having a righteousness of my own that comes from the law, but that which is through faith in Christ .... I want to know Christ and the power of his resurrection *and the fellowship of sharing in his sufferings, becoming like him in his death*" (Philippians 3:8-10, italics added).

Sharing (*koinonia*) in his sufferings—when Christ died something amazing happened. He became God's eternal sacrifice. All those lambs and goats, bulls, turtledoves and pigeons that had been slaughtered over the centuries were now obsolete. That seemingly endless flow of blood from tabernacle and temple could now stop because an eternal substitute had arrived.

"When this priest," Hebrews explains, "had offered for all time one sacrifice for sins, he sat down at the right hand of God. Since that time he waits for his enemies to be made his footstool, because by one sacrifice he has made perfect forever those who are being made holy" (Hebrews 10:12-14).

Something amazing indeed! "We have confidence to enter the Most Holy Place by the blood of Jesus, by a new and living way, opened for us through the curtain, that is, his body" (Hebrews 10:19-20). Before this, no one could approach God's glorious presence. Now the least and lowliest sinners who by faith apply the Lamb's blood to the doorposts of their hearts are welcome in the throne room of the King. No waiting, no begging, no reservations required. No need to make large campaign donations or know the *right people.* This party is open to whoever accepts God's gracious invitation.

In fact, your main qualification is to recognize you have no qualifications. "Not having a righteousness of my own," Paul insists, "but that which is through faith in Christ."

Just as I am without one plea,
But that Thy blood was shed for me,

And that Thou bidst me come to Thee,
O Lamb of God, I come.

That's it! That's the gospel. Nobody could open the scroll until the Lamb came along. Only He could reclaim for us our inheritance as children of God. In Him we who've made perfect messes of our lives are *made perfect forever.* "You are in Christ Jesus, who has become for us wisdom from God—that is, our righteousness, holiness and redemption" (1 Corinthians 1:30). So if you're going to brag, Paul continues, do all your bragging about the Lord.

The Blood of the Lamb. That's our secret weapon #1 against Satan's evil powers. The devil had us enslaved like those pathetic Israelites in Egypt. We were helpless and hopeless. Then the Lamb shed His blood and the chains of darkness were snapped like old shoestrings. Now God doesn't see our sins; He just sees Christ. We're residents in God's promised land, and old Pharaoh Lucifer can't lay a hand on us anymore. Hallelujah! We've overcome him by the blood of *the* Passover Lamb.

Remember that the only requirement was that the blood be applied to the door posts. The death angel did not check on how the inhabitants of the house were dressed. He did not grade the wife on her housekeeping skills. He needed to check on only one thing, the blood on the doorpost.

Former first lady Rosalynn Carter tells an intriguing story. After President Jimmy Carter left the White House, he and she were traveling in Brazil. There Governor Leonel Brizzola and his two granddaughters greeted them with flowers and tears. Brizzola was too emotional to utter a word.

Later the Carters learned the origin of their extraordinary reception. During Carter's administration, Brizzola had learned he was to be arrested in exile and returned to Brazil for imprisonment and possible execution. He contacted the

U.S. Embassy for help on a Friday and was told to come back on Monday after embassy officials had contacted the President. By Monday, however, Brizzola had frantically phoned the embassy to say his home was surrounded by soldiers, and he was under their authority.

"No," he was told emphatically, "as of now you are under the authority of the President of the United States."

"At that moment," Brizzola told the Carters, "I was saved."

We understand that story, don't we? Sin had us surrounded. Cut off. Doomed. Then Christ reached out to where we were in exile and put us under the authority of His redeeming work. The enemy could no longer touch us. It's too wonderful for words.

Secret Weapon #2—Speak the Word

"... And by the Word of their testimony." That's the second secret weapon at our disposal.

This has nothing to do with people giving their personal testimonies. If our personal recounting of our spiritual journeys are what we're relying on to fight the devil, we are trying to tame tigers with toothpicks. The Bible (*logos*) is what Revelation 12:11 means. The Word of God is our word of testimony. That's what we're called to testify to and about.

The Word was in the beginning, says John 1. The Word was with God. The Word *was* God. The Word made everything that's ever been made. The Word was life and light. One day that Word became flesh and made His dwelling among us. That One and Only came as God's Lamb, and even in that guise His glory shone like a Tiffany diamond in a discount store.

Heaven and earth will pass away, but God's Word will never pass away (Matthew 24:35). It's like a rock you can build your life on and the floods cannot destroy you (Matthew 7:24-27).

Or a super-sharpened, double-edged sword that slices through to the heart and lays everything bare before God. Or a seed that miraculously germinates new life in the stubborn soil of sinful souls. *This* word of testimony is a nuclear bomb armed to detonate in the middle of Satan's strongholds.

Thank God that our faith isn't theoretical or speculative. It is authoritative. Our belief rides on the back of an infallible Book which reveals an infallible God. You can't find anything bigger or better or surer than this with which to face life and eternity. With the author of Romans we exclaim, "Oh, the depth of the riches of the wisdom and knowledge of God! How unsearchable his judgments, and his paths beyond tracing out! ... For from him and through him and to him are all things. To him be the glory forever! Amen" (Romans 12:33, 36).

Lloyd C. Douglas, author of *The Robe*, lived in a boarding house while attending university. Downstairs from him on the first floor resided a retired music teacher. The man was too feeble to leave his apartment, so Douglas made a point of checking in on him every day.

They followed this ritual. Douglas would open the old teacher's door and ask, "What's the good news today?" Picking up his tuning fork and tapping it on the side of his wheelchair, the man would reply, "That's middle C! It was middle C yesterday; it will be middle C tomorrow; it will be middle C a thousand years from now. The tenor upstairs sings flat, the piano across the hall is out of tune, but *that* is middle C!"

God and His Word function as our middle C, the one unshakable constant in a shook-up world.

The weapon is the *spoken* word. Two New Testament words are translated "word" in our English Bibles. The word *logos* is the word used in John 1. Jesus is the Living Logos. The Bible is the Written Logos. Logos refers to the total revealed Word of God.

The second word is *rhema*. This is the word used here in Revelation 12. It is also the word used in Ephesians 6 to identify "the sword of the Spirit." While these words are used almost interchangeably, the word *rhema* is used for the spoken word. In Scripture the *rhema* comes from the *logos*, but it is a special word for a special time of need. Jesus used the *rhema* in His encounter with the devil in His wilderness temptation. When He said, "It is written...," He then lifted the correct *rhema* out of the *logos* to repel the Tempter.

The Word of God is the Sword of the Spirit. It is the Word of our testimony. It is the Weapon of Winners. We overcome by this mighty weapon.

Secret Weapon #3—Shout Victory

The word *rejoice* in verse 12 comes from two words meaning "big voice." A good translation would be "shout." All heaven is invited to shout. Rejoice! Celebrate the victory! This is one of the most potent weapons of conquering saints. Paul exhorts, "Rejoice in the Lord always. I will say it again, Rejoice!" (Philippians 4:4).

Some believers do not enjoy the victory they should because they have not learned to shout. Shouting victory is a weapon used both in the Old Testament and the New. In several instances victory came only when God's people shouted.

Israel had just crossed the Jordan River. They had arrived in the Promised Land, the inheritance Jehovah had promised. But immediately they ran up against a walled city—Jericho. This motley band of ex-slaves was ill-prepared to do battle with the defenders of this city. Joshua was perturbed and perplexed. He had no idea how they were to take this God-given possession.

As he walked around the city, he encountered a stranger. Pulling his sword he challenged, "Who are you? Are you friend or foe?" The stranger replied, "I am Captain of the Lord's Host. I have come to direct the battle."

Joshua then inquired about the battle plan.

The stranger offered a simple plan—march and shout. The heirs to this promised land were to march around the walls of this seemingly impregnable city for seven days—once each day for six days and seven times on the seventh day. Jehovah gave them something they could do. If He had told them to storm the gates of the city with battering rams, they were not equipped to do that. But they could march.

Imagine what must have happened. These weary pilgrims started walking. In perfect obedience they circled the city the first day—nothing changed. The second day—nothing changed. The third ... the fourth ... the fifth—still everything was the same. Someone must have muttered, "Come on, Joshua, this is silly. Look at those soldiers on the wall laughing at us. We are wasting our time."

"Shut up," Joshua yelled, "keep walking!"

They completed the walk on the sixth day and began preparations for the arduous journey on the seventh day. Rising early and struggling through the marathon journey of the seventh day, they saw absolutely no sign of victory. Though walking in perfect obedience, there were no visible results of God's battle plan.

Grumbling and complaining, they trudged on, circling the city seven times on that last day. Not one sign of any supernatural help. No indication of victory.

But, there was one final weapon in their battle plan—they were to shout.

Nothing happened until they shouted. But when they shouted, the walls fell into the ground and the city fell to the people of God. What if they had not shouted? What if they had caved to the taunting? What if they had obeyed all the orders given by the Captain except the command to shout?

I wonder how many cities fortified and occupied by the enemy would fall if God's people learned to shout victory. Not just anytime. Shouting alone would never have taken Jericho. The marching in silence was essential preparation for the shouting. But there comes a time when God's victorious army must shout (Joshua, chs. 5, 6).

Gideon's victory is another example of the power of shouting. Gideon was chosen by God to bring deliverance to Israel. The Midianites were encamped like a horde of grasshoppers in the valley. Gideon and his 300 men stood on the mountains around the valley. What was to be the weapon they were to use? They all had pitchers, torches and trumpets. Their orders were to break the pitchers, lift the torches high, and blow the trumpets. All this at the command of Gideon. But when did the victory come? When they shouted!

Listen to their declaration, "The Sword of the Lord and of Gideon!" They shouted victory and God gave it. The Midianites destroyed each other (Judges, chs. 6, 7).

Then, there is the story of Paul and Silas in Philippi (Acts 16). They had been thrust into jail for exorcising the demons that possessed a girl and thus disrupting a thriving business in sorcery.

Imagine the scene: It's midnight. The two apostles are in the maximum security section of the prison. Paul says, "Silas, I feel like shouting!" Silas whispers, "Paul, you had better keep quiet. These are mean dudes in this cell. You disturb them in the middle of the night and we may not get out of here alive."

"But I tell you, Silas," Paul retorts, "I feel like praising the Lord!" Paul was sensing the call to shout victory. Never mind the time of day (or night). What does it matter that the cell mates are not in tune with the music? "Let's sing praises to

God!" Paul shouts and begins to sing.

The results speak for themselves. Earthquake! Doors fly open! Jailer repents! Baptismal service before daybreak! All because Paul and Silas knew how to shout.

The Crux of Communion

This is what the Lord's Supper is about: celebrating the blood of the Lamb and the Word of our testimony. It is a communion of conquerors, those who've overcome the enemy of their souls by trusting in Christ's vicarious death and life-changing truth. The elements of communion are basic yet graphic. The cup Christians drink symbolizes that covering blood, and the bread images the soul-nourishing Word. They constantly remind us who we are. They define us as believers.

"I am the living bread that came down from heaven," Jesus told an incredulous crowd in the Capernaum synagogue (John 6). "If a man eats of this bread, he will live forever. This bread is my flesh, which I will give for the life of the world."

"How can this man give us his flesh to eat?" some of them scoffed.

Jesus retorted, "Whoever eats my flesh and drinks my blood has eternal life, and I will raise him up at the last day. For my flesh is real food and my blood is real drink." It was more than many of His disciples could swallow, and they left Him in droves. "You do not want to leave too, do you?" He plaintively asked the Twelve.

For once, impetuous Peter got it right. "Lord, to whom shall we go? You have the words of eternal life. We believe and know that you are the Holy One of God." That's the Christian faith in a nutshell.

The Lord's Supper is the New Testament Passover, the church's perpetual reminder of its liberation from "Egypt" by the sovereign act of God. "Remember," God urges us. "Always remember what has saved you." In eating and drinking, we reenact the slaying of God's innocent Lamb and our journey from slavery to salvation; we experience the "fellowship of his suffering." Through these actions we also foreshadow God's final triumph over all the Pharaohs and Egypts of darkness. We anticipate those magnificent Revelation scenes when faith becomes sight and reality replaces ritual. "Whenever you eat this bread and drink this cup, you proclaim the Lord's death until he comes" (1 Corinthians 11:26).

The cup—the blood of the Lamb. The bread—the Word of our testimony. By these we overcome the devil. Through these we find the courage to face death without shrinking. For the Lamb has suffered death for us, and the "sting" of death which is sin no longer threatens us.

Go ahead, weary warrior. Remove the load from your shoulders. You don't have to overcome by your good works, or your good intentions, or your feelings, or your ability to handle stress, or your rigorous devotional life, or your good track record. On your own you're as impotent and pitiful as those Hebrew slaves. But it's okay for you to be weak—that's when His strength really shines. You win the battle against Satan by relying not on who you are but who He is. Not on what you can do but what He has done. Quit sweating and fretting. Rest in His provisions, His blood and His bread.

So many sincere Christians miss the point. They approach the Lord's table focusing on their performance rather than God's. They torment themselves questioning whether they're worthy to participate. While self-reflection and penitence are important, the chief focus of communion is God's worthiness rather than ours. Of course we're not deserving. Jesus Christ is, though, and the spotlight of the Lord's Supper shines on Him. It's a time for toasting victory rather than bemoaning defeat.

Feast on the scenes of that amazing final word to the Word. Revelation portrays a Lion who is also Lamb, a Creator who became created, and a King who lived and died as a pauper. In these paradoxes shines the jeweled truth of our Savior/Lord. F. W. Pitt's "Maker of the Universe" captures the divine enigma:

The Maker of the Universe
As Man, for man was made a curse.
The claims of Law which He had made,
Unto the uttermost He paid.

His holy fingers made the bough
Which grew the thorns that crowned His brow.
The nails that pierced His hands were mined
In secret places He designed.

He made the forest whence there sprung
The tree on which His body hung.
He died upon a cross of wood,
Yet made the hill on which it stood.

The sky that darkened o'er His head
By Him above the earth was spread.
The sun that hid from Him its face
By His decree was poised in space.

The spear which spilled His precious blood
Was tempered in the fires of God.
The grave in which His form was laid,
Was hewn in rocks His hands had made.

The throne on which He now appears

Was His from everlasting years.
But a new glory crowns His brow,
And every knee to Him shall bow.

Pause amid the mist and shadows. Wonder at the Word who became a Lamb.

Wonder, worship, and rejoice! Stand on the blood, speak the Word, and shout the victory! These are the secret weapons of the conquerors.

Hell is not compatible with God's love; it is a direct consequence of it.

—E. L. Mascall

God determines human destiny. Whatever other powers we may meet in this life, God's power is final. He has the last word.

—Bruce Shelley

It is inappropriate, then, for Christians to lead hangdog, browbeaten, downtrodden lives. That kind of fatalistic behavior is appropriate to the vanquished, the losers—but we who are in Christ are as certain of triumph as is Christ whom we serve.

—Charles Conn

12 The Final Victory

From a human viewpoint the battle of good versus evil is not faring well. War, famine, drought, disease, terrorism, torture, and other monsters prowl the international landscape. Crime and corruption and immorality and injustice plague local communities. Divorce, abuse, and alienation haunt the family. While Christians want to believe God's promises that a better day is coming and that the scales of justice will finally balance, sometimes those assurances seem pale against the backdrop of present realities.

Like the writer of Psalm 73, the believer's feet almost slip on the path of faith, for the truth upon which our faith is based appears mocked by the arrogance and prosperity of the wicked. With suffering saints of the past we find ourselves crying, "How long, O Lord, how long ...?"

Back to the Future

That's why the prophecy of Revelation looms so large on the biblical landscape. It provides a window overlooking eternity, a time ship that transports the believer forward to give beleaguered souls a welcome glimpse of God's final victory. Of Satan's ultimate defeat. Of the irrevocable triumph of all that is right and good and true over everything that is wrong and bad and false.

No chapter of Revelation offers a bigger feast for the eyes of faith than chapter 20. Here hangs the divine portrait of evil's final undoing. Here for our viewing is what He "who is, and who was, and who is to come" already sees perfectly. Here is Satan's ultimate day of reckoning.

CNN may take us instantaneously across the world for "breaking news," but only God can take us across the eons to show us sin-breaking news. Glue your eyes to heaven's channel for this breathtaking scene:

> And I saw an angel coming down out of heaven, having the key to the Abyss and holding in his hand a great chain. He seized the dragon, that ancient serpent, who is the devil, or Satan, and bound him for a thousand years. He threw him into the Abyss, and locked and sealed it over him, to keep him from deceiving the nations any more until the thousand years were ended. After that, he must be set free for a short time.

I saw thrones on which were seated those who had been given authority to judge. And I saw the souls of those who had been beheaded because of their testimony for Jesus and because of the word of God. They had not worshiped the beast or his image and had not received his mark on their foreheads or their hands. They came to life and reigned with Christ a thousand years. (The rest of the dead did not come to life until the thousand years were ended.) This is the first resurrection. Blessed and holy are those who have part in the first resurrection. The second death has no power over them, but they will be priests of God and of Christ and will reign with him for a thousand years.

When the thousand years are over, Satan will be released from his prison and will go out to deceive the nations in the four corners of the earth—Gog and Magog—to gather them for battle. In number they are like the sand on the seashore. They marched across the breadth of the earth and surrounded the camp of God's people, the city he loves. But fire came down from heaven and devoured them. And the devil, who deceived them, was thrown into the lake of burning sulfur, where the beast and the false prophet had been thrown. They will be tormented day and night for ever and ever.

Then I saw a great white throne and him who was seated on it. Earth and sky fled from his presence, and there was no place for them. And I saw the dead, great and small, standing before the throne, and books were opened. Another book was opened, which is the book of life. The dead were judged according to what they had done as recorded in the books. The sea gave up the dead that were in them, and each person was judged according to what he had done. Then death and Hades were thrown into the lake of fire. The lake of fire is the second death. If anyone's name was not found written in the book of life, he was thrown into the lake of fire.

Evil's Last Gasp

You're watching iniquity's last gasp. The problem of evil, the questions regarding its origin, the consternation regarding God's allowing it to continue—all those haunting philosophical and theological riddles are resolved in this chapter. There are no more missing pieces to the puzzle. The picture stands complete.

First, the chapter tells us God is going to give lost humanity one final chance to turn to Him after the Church is snatched away by Christ. Satan will be bound so he cannot deceive the nations. He whose hand has sown all the seeds of sin and sorrow and suffering this world reaps, is placed on death row. God's plan of restoration, "as he promised long ago through his holy prophets" (Acts 3:21), is approaching its final stages.

The Bible has great news for you. You're not going to lose a thing. Nothing which has been forfeited due to the fall of humanity will remain that way. In fact, God's eternal life insurance policy states that, when He completes His reclamation of what the fiend wrecked, the result will exceed even Eden's pre-fall paradise. Now that's *replacement* insurance. The ledger's bottom line will be a surplus, not a deficit, and part of the settling of accounts will be dealing with the devil.

Though Satan has persisted, he had to know from the moment he first felt heaven's boot that his doom was certain. Like a badly-overmatched boxer, he's been knocked to the canvas repeatedly. "How you have fallen from heaven, O morning star, son of the dawn" (Isaiah 14:12). "I saw Satan fall like lightning from heaven" (Luke 10:18). "The great dragon was hurled down" (Revelation 12:9).

When Jesus died and rose again, He landed the knockout blow. As God had assured a devastated Adam and Eve, the offspring of a woman crunched the serpent's head beneath his heel.

Now, Revelation 20 pictures that old snake being cast down into "the Abyss," imprisoned for a thousand years for a taste of the punishment awaiting him. Then God releases him to test earth's inhabitants one more time, to see if they will finally bow the knee to Him. Most don't. Instead they enlist in the traitor's army for one final thrust against their Sovereign. The attack, however, ends before it begins, with a fiery blast from heaven's nostrils.

Then Satan is given a long-overdue lake vacation. The bad news for him is that it's a lake of fire, and his trip isn't a vacation but permanent retirement. Sharing his fate are his legions of demons and every person whose "name was not found written in the book of life." It is an awesome scene.

Hell Isn't Meant for You

We don't hear much preaching about hell these days. Folks consider it impolite, like telling the details of one's gall bladder surgery at the dinner table. Admittedly, preachers sometimes abused the topic in the past. We shouldn't throw out the Bible with the blatherers, however. Hell is a reality. Among the people who've believed in it is Jesus. In His ministry, He talked about it constantly.

He has great news for us in that regard, however. We don't belong in hell. According to His words in Matthew 25:41, hell is for the devil and his angels. The Lord did not intend for a single human being to end up in eternal torment. In fact, He has been working overtime, since Adam and Eve sinned, to keep you and me out of the place. On the cross He even went so far as to experience hell Himself for us. Those who become eternally damned will have to run God's red lights and roadblocks every mile of their way.

Nevertheless some will complete the trip. The final toll booth on the road to perdition is pictured here as a great white throne. So imposing is the One who sits on it that everyone and everything shrinks from His presence. No wonder. He possesses a flawless record of every person's words, actions, and motives. Everything you've ever done in violation of God's laws, every rejection of Christ's love, every selfish tendency, every mean-spirited thought—it's all in the celestial database.

Unless ... Unless you've made a simple transaction in advance. It's so simple a fool could do it, and so inexpensive the poorest could afford it. All that's required is to go to that Judge and say, "I'm guilty of everything that's recorded about me. I don't have an excuse. I plead guilty. However, I understand Your Son has already paid the penalty for those crimes. He's served my time. I can't comprehend why He would have done such a thing for somebody like me, but since He's offered me this priceless gift, Sir, I throw myself upon the mercy of Your court and ask You to accept His punishment for my wrongs."

When you do that, two marvelous things happen. First the Judge immediately enters your name in another record called "the Book of Life." Then He expunges all the other records. With a punch of the key, those files are erased. The only entry to be found under your name is three words long, in bold red letters: *paid in full.*

If you have made that transaction, you needn't concern yourself about the great white throne judgment described in Revelation 20. You won't even be there, unless perhaps as an observer. The Judge might invite you for that, since He's now your best Friend. And if you were, and anyone accused you of anything or demanded that your records be made public, you'd have no cause for worry. The facts are all there—or rather not there, and your name in that book of life is the final piece of evidence. Case closed. Court's adjourned.

How awful that some people won't have their names in that book! How tragic that some recklessly ran every roadblock and ignored every love note of warning. If anything should spur us as Christians to evangelize the world, this is it. It should terrify us to picture family or friends or neighbors or coworkers or any human being who was never intended for hell, facing that eternal horror of lostness and godlessness and hopelessness. Doesn't this scene stir you?

It stirs God. It's the Father's brokenhearted passion to see His prodigal children come back home. Even as this final page of the Bible closes, the Lord is trying to sell more tickets on the gospel train. "The Spirit and the bride say, 'Come!' And let him who hears say, 'Come!' Whoever is thirsty, let him come; and whoever wishes, let him take the free gift of the water of life" (Revelation 22:17).

"Come!" pleads our Lord and Savior, because He doesn't want ever to have to say "Go away; I never knew you." He despises the thought of it. That's why He remains so patient with villainous humanity, "not wanting anyone to perish, but everyone to come to repentance" (2 Peter 3:9). *Everyone!*

A Vanquished Foe

As for Satan, his destiny is decided. God has fixed a special place for him and his co-conspirators. Whether the description, "lake of fire and sulphur" (RSV, NEB), is literal or metaphoric is insignificant; they will be "tormented day and night for ever and ever."

And as for the dung god's handiwork, the Creator remains determined to remove all the blots, briers, and booby traps in His marred creation. He will liberate it "from its bondage to decay" and bring it "into the glorious freedom of the children of God" (Romans 8:21). Only a few words past that horrific sight of the lake of fire we see these salving words, "They will be his people, and God himself will be with them and be their God. He will wipe every tear from their eyes. There will be no more death or mourning or crying or pain, for the old order of things has passed away" (Revelation 21:3-4).

Can you imagine it? No more death. No more sorrow. No more fear. No more suffering. No more sin. No more trouble. No more depression or guilt or loneliness or hatred or broken-heartedness. Every fingerprint of the fall has been wiped away.

Even now we get a taste of the final triumph of God and His followers. Already He dwells with us through His Spirit, who is a deposit guaranteeing our future inheritance. Already we have constant access to the King of kings. Already we are adopted into God's family. Already we're children of God, John marvels (1 John 3:2), and we don't even have a clear picture yet of what we will be when He gets through with us. We do know this much: we'll be just like Jesus, and the Spirit has already begun that transformation. Yes, the kingdom worker's benefits package is huge.

One foretaste of our final fate, and the devil's, is the power God gives us over him, even to cast out demons. As Jesus told that motley crew of Galilean disciples, "I have given you authority to trample on snakes and scorpions and to overcome all the power of the enemy; nothing will harm you." The church's mission is to plunder hell by the power of God, snatching souls from his fiery clutches and retaking territory he's usurped. According to Matthew 16, not even the gates of hell can withstand its advances.

"The reason the Son of God appeared was to destroy the devil's work" (1 John 3:8). Christians aren't to run or hide from the devil. We're to go after his hangouts, to invade his house, to recover his hostages. Armed with the authority and weapons Christ gives us, we should meet him head-on. Our mission to the enslaved is the same as the one Jesus presented to Paul, "to open their eyes and turn them from darkness to light, and from the power of Satan to God, so that they may receive forgiveness of sins and a place among those who are sanctified by faith in me" (Acts 26:18).

Plundering hell is our mission. God is our might. Eternal souls are our motivation.

It's Over

Baseball manager Casey Stengel was famous for mangling the language. His many "Stengelisms" endeared the crusty skipper to the sporting public. One of his well-known malapropisms is "It ain't over 'til it's over," meaning the outcome of a game is still in doubt until the final out.

The Bible goes one better than Casey. It reports that, in the contest between good and evil, it's over *before* it's over. Human history may still have innings to play, but the game is no longer in doubt. God has won. The victory is ours.

Jesus Christ said it first. A helpless Lamb on a Roman cross, bleeding and suffocating before a hostile crowd, He wet His lips for a proclamation of victory. It was the cry of a champion. In a surprisingly loud voice he exclaimed, "It is finished!" He didn't mean that He was done for, or that His suffering was mercifully drawing to a close. He meant His salvation work was finished. He had whipped the enemy of our souls once and for all.

This is the Easter message. This is our reason for existence as the church. We don't worship and serve God merely because we admire the Christian value system, or find it a fascinating theory, or see it as a neat bit of history, or think it will make our lives go a little better. No! We worship and serve Him because of a finished product. A turnkey job. A historical reality that transcends and befuddles history.

We're the kind of people who desperately need that reality. Our lives are anything but finished. Looking at ourselves we see weaknesses, flaws, sins, failures, fears. But God says, "It's over. I've won your victory for you. I know that sometimes it doesn't seem like it and there are battles left to fight, but you can take this to the bank. It is finished!"

Go ahead, fellow soldier, and enjoy your victory. Your diploma has been printed and your cap and gown are waiting. Your inheritance is drawing interest in heaven's bank. The banquet hall has been decorated. Your reservation at the ball is confirmed. Your eternal dwelling place has been built and furnished. Your winner's trophy already has your name carved on it.

We aren't through making mistakes yet, but one day we will be.

We're not very much like Jesus yet, but one day we shall be.

Life isn't fair, but it will be.

All the wrongs haven't been righted, but they will be.

All the diseases haven't been banished, but one day they will be.

Satan has not yet been tossed on God's eternal trash pile, but it will happen.

All the broken hearts haven't been healed, but they're going to be.

Death hasn't been destroyed, but its end will come.

All our tears haven't been wiped away yet, but on that day God will do it with His own loving hand.

All the stones that entomb and entrap us haven't yet been rolled out of the way, but the One who rolled away the rock from Jesus' grave is going to do it.

The war is drawing to a close, but the victory party's just getting started.

The scene is heaven. Near God's throne. Very near.

A dazzling, jewel-like figure stands bathed in light, leading the worship of the Almighty and proclaiming His greatness. The worshiper is splendid. Full of beauty, grace, and wisdom. Perfect in every way.

Yet he seems oblivious to his beauty. Gazing at the majestic occupant of the throne, he raises a mellifluous voice in song. Amid a sound like cascading waterfalls, the words ring clear: "Worthy is the Lamb, who was slain, to receive power and wealth and strength and honor and glory and praise."

Who is this brilliant creature touching the skirts of God's glory?

It once was Lucifer. Long, long ago. Before his tragic mutiny. Now someone else fills those Shekinah-shined shoes.

Take a closer look. Can you tell who it is?

His name is Multitude. Her name is Throng. It is not one worshiper, but many. From every race and language and people and nation. All of them prophets and priests and kings. All of them praising and serving the Lord of all.

He knows them by another name, though. He calls them Sons of the morning. Daughters of light. He gave them those titles. He remade them into the beautiful creatures that surround His presence with praise. They adore Him day and night, for they owe Him everything they have become.

Now do you know who this is standing before the throne of God?

It is you.

It is I.

The war of all wars is over. Hallelujah! Satan has been crushed. God has won.

We have won.

Bibliography

Alexander, William Menzies, *Demonic Possession in the New Testament*, Grand Rapids, Baker Book House, Reprinted 1980 from the 1902 edition.

Barnhouse, Donald Grey, *The Invisible War*, Grand Rapids, Zondervan Publishing House, 1965.

Bounds, E. M., *Winning the Invisible War*, Springdale, PA, Whitaker House, 1984.

Bounds, E. M., *Satan, His Personality, Power and Overthrow*, Grand Rapids, Baker Book House, Reprinted 1972.

Conn, Charles W., *The Anatomy of Evil*, Old Tappan, NJ, Fleming H. Revell Company, 1981.

Dawson, John, *Taking Our Cities for God*, Lake Mary, FL, Creation House, 1989.

Dickason, C. Fred, *Demon Possession and the Christian*, Westchester, IL, Crossway Books, 1987 (originally published by Moody Bible Institute).

Huegel, F. J., *That Old Serpent The DEVIL*, Grand Rapids, Zondervan Publishing House, 1954.

Huegel, F. J., *The Mystery of Iniquity*, Minneapolis, Bethany Fellowship, Inc., 1968.

Koch, Kurt, *Demonology Past and Present*, Grand Rapids, Kregel Publications, 1973.

Lewis, C. S., *The Screwtape Letters*, New York, Macmillan, 1943.

Lindsell, Harold, *The World, the Flesh, and the Devil*, Washington, DC, Canon Press, 1973.

Montgomery, John Warwick, ed., *Demon Possession*, Minneapolis, Bethany House Publishers, 1976.

Morgan, G. Campbell, *The Voice of the Devil*, New York, Fleming H. Revell Company, date unknown.

Ness, Alexander William, *Transference of Spirits*, Downsview, Ontario, Canada, Agapre Publications, Inc., 1984.

Nevius, John L., *Demon Possession*, Grand Rapids, Kregel Publications, 1968 (originally published under the title *Demon Possession and Allied Themes* in 1894 by Fleming H. Revell Company).

Sherman, Dean, *Spiritual Warfare For Every Christian*, Seattle, YWAM Publishing, 1990.

Sumrall, Lester, *Demons, The Answer Book*, Nashville, Thomas Nelson Publishers, 1979.

Thielicke, Helmut, *Between God and Satan*, Grand Rapids, Wm. B. Eerdmans Publishing Company, 1958.

Unger, Merrill, *Biblical Demonology*, Wheaton, IL, Scripture Press, 1952.

Unger, Merrill, *What Demons Can Do to Saints*, Chicago, Moody Press, 1977.